CORPORATE

Anointing

Christ: Manifest in the Fullness of His Body

Kelley Varner

Destiny Image ® Publishers, Inc.
P.O. Box 310
Shippensburg, PA 17257-0310

"We Publish the Prophets"

ISBN 0-7684-2011-3

For Worldwide Distribution
Printed in the U.S.A.

Third Printing: 2000   Fourth Printing: 2002

This book and all other Destiny Image, Revival Press, MercyPlace, Fresh Bread, Destiny Image Fiction, and Treasure House books are available at Christian bookstores and distributors worldwide.

For a U.S. bookstore nearest you, call **1-800-722-6774**.
For more information on foreign distributors, call **717-532-3040**.
Or reach us on the Internet: **www.destinyimage.com**

Dedication

There are two primary apothecaries that have forever changed and shaped my life and ministry: my family and my local church.

To Joann, my friend and companion for 25 years; and to April, Jonathan, Joy Beth, and David, each unique and outrageously special. I live and breathe in the heavenlies. You have brought me back down to earth and taught me about life. You have shown me how to love people.

To the elders, deacons, and saints of Praise Tabernacle. You each have spiced my life with your own. You are a blessing to the Lord, to me, to my family, and to this ministry. The anointing that I carry is the anointing of our whole house. My voice is our voice. Our reward shall be great.

Acknowledgments

To prophet Lynn Hiles, for giving me fresh inspiration concerning the corporate anointing.

To Don Nori and the editorial team at Destiny Image, for their wisdom and skill in formatting this manuscript. A special thanks to Larry Walker and his gift of writing. Indeed, this book itself is the fruit of corporate anointing.

To the Holy Spirit, who is my Teacher.

About the Cover

From the moment I started reading this manuscript, two things began to happen: I started seeing pictures and I started taking notes. The Lord opened up this message of *corporate anointing* so vividly to me that I couldn't write down the insights I was receiving fast enough. And as I started to seek God for a cover design, an idea came almost instantly (which isn't always the case). I wanted to mirror the word pictures that Pastor Varner painted so clearly in the text, and the shofar pouring out the anointing oil perfectly symbolizes the beginning of our walk into corporate anointing. The grapes also portray that corporate anointing—each individually containing the "new wine" that must flow out corporately. I challenge you to see yourself "poured out" as part of that *Corporate Anointing*.

Tony Laidig
Artist, Destiny Image

Table of Contents

Foreword

In 1992, the Lord spoke a clear word to me. "I am about to wrestle control of the Church out of the hands of arrogant and insecure men. I will return it to the hands of My Son, who alone knows how to build His Church."

These were sobering words indeed. But He was not through. "Whatever I am toppling, do not attempt to prop up. What I am about to do is much bigger than one man. It is much weightier than one man can carry. I want a Body in whom I can rest."

We are just beginning to see the fulfillment of these words today. The next few years will be times of incredible change and unparalleled opportunity to experience His presence and His corporate anointing like never before in history. We will be challenged to the core of our tradition and pushed to the far reaches of our faith.

He will clear our hearts and our motives until we can truly see unity as all of His people gathered unto Him and not unto our individual doctrinal beliefs. For what God is about to do is even bigger than our doctrine. It is not bigger than truth, but it is bigger than our doctrine.

In this anointing, the plans of carnal man are consumed in the breath of His Spirit. Here, man's ego and personal ambition are consumed by the "devouring fire" of Isaiah 33:14 and all that remains is the brokenness of man's yieldedness to His purposes in the earth.

In this dimension of His glory, men dare not interject opinion or objection. They neither vie for attention nor feel rejection at His silence. The Lord may do what He wants, when He wants, and with whom He wants in the setting He wants. Those yielded to this anointing can only rejoice that His glory is displayed in the earth, whether or not the Lord happened to use them at the moment. His glory is the principal thing, for the passion of the corporate anointing is His glory. It is only the corporate anointing that will bring His glory to the earth.

Renewal and revival have begun in a tremendous way. The Lord is breaking down dividing walls for a specific purpose. The walls between denominations, ethnic groups, nations, genders, and races are walls that must come down for His glory to flow freely throughout the earth. But the formidable religious wall between clergy and laity must also come down for the fullness of the Lord Jesus to be seen in the earth. The corporate anointing is the fullest expression of Jesus Christ. This is the Christ that the nations will run to. This is the Christ that will be a light to the nations and that will carry the good news to the four corners of the earth.

The corporate anointing of the Lord has the uniqueness to show the world the glory of an invisible God through a body, with every part working in such unison that the glory of the anointing outshines the ego of man. But this anointing also has the ability to recognize the importance and value of the individual without disrupting the display of His presence in the many-membered expression of the Lord Jesus. Only God can accomplish such a thing. And He will, through simple folk like you and I who have no other desire or passion but to see Him and to experience the full salvation of the Lord.

This book is the first major prophetic work that describes the function and power of the Anointed One, the mighty Lord of Hosts among His people. It is where we must go if we are to continue to flow in all that God is giving us.

The corporate anointing is us, but it begins with me. O God, open my heart, revive me not just to revelation, but to change. Do not just illumine Your word, but write it on my heart, that I may become what I believe; and that I may be one of many who will carry Your glory in the corporate anointing.

Don Nori, Publisher
Destiny Image Publishers

Preface

Kelley Varner has been my brother and friend ever since we grew up together in the mountains of West Virginia. We cut our spiritual teeth on the same foundational ministries. He and I are outrageous composites of every man or woman of God who ever graced our lives. We exemplify the work of the greatest Apothecary of all times: the Lord Jesus Christ.

For many years Kelley Varner has greatly blessed the Body of Christ with numerous inspired writings that teach present and progressive truth. These volumes have forever changed the minds and lives of us who have read them. They constitute an outstanding resource of study material to men and women who seek after something beyond the typical Babylonian bologna so often offered on the tables of confused Christianity.

Pastor Varner has unselfishly given himself to the Word of God and to his Teacher, the Holy Spirit. From his wealthy storehouse, which has been such a constant asset to the

Church at large, there now comes his latest publication, a fresh impartation concerning "corporate anointing."

Many ministries are marked by a self-centered and self-seeking posture. They know nothing of losing sight of "me" and "mine" to become part of an "us." The book before you breathes fresh direction for the future. The Church is in uncharted waters, and we must experience apostolic and prophetic instruction that will bring us into our personal and corporate destinies.

Each of us has accomplished much with his individual anointing. What could happen if we dwelled together in unity, the mixing bowl of compound anointing? These meaningful relationships would release the anointing from the Head that flows down to the skirts of His garments (Ps. 133). May we be the ones who will see the brethren reconciled! God has commanded blessing in the place of unity, even life evermore.

We all are a people of compound substance, ingredients that must be poured from vessel to vessel. Then, collectively, we will finally set forth the all-together loveliness of the corporate Christ. But if we continue in the selfish ways of our own individual agendas, His Body will remain fragmented, an eye or hand here, a foot there. His visage and image will be marred as His bones stay disjointed (Ps. 22:14; Is. 52:14).

The days ahead will be challenging. The church in the wilderness was our example (1 Cor. 10:11). In the Old Testament, "they" passed through the Red Sea by faith (Heb. 11:29). It is time for each one to take his place in the Body of Christ, the holy nation, the family and people of God. Bring your spice. Mingle your life and ministry with others. Come up higher into the One whose name is like ointment poured forth (Song 1:3).

Get your Bible and prepare your heart. Learn fresh truth from this seasoned teacher. Then submit to your heavenly Priest who alone can stir and blend each life into the divine pot.

There is an anointing oil on all of us that is far greater than the anointing on any one of us—the "corporate anointing" will destroy creation's yoke of bondage!

Prophet Lynn Hiles
Word of Deliverance Church
Berkeley Springs, West Virginia

Introduction

For the most part, American Christendom is entertainment-based, need-oriented, and man-centered. We are obsessed with the *hand* of God—what He can do for us. Like children, we are more interested in His presents than His presence. Most ministries are platform-based. We Christians are content to sit by, cheering on the "man of God" or the "woman of God" to do his or her thing while we faithfully fellowship with the back of somebody's head once or twice a week.

Individual accomplishments are not bad. The "faith points" of the personal life and ministry of Moses, one of the most anointed individuals in the Bible, is highlighted in the Book of Hebrews.

By faith "he" refused to be called the son of Pharaoh's daughter.

By faith "he" had respect unto the reward of obedience.

By faith "he" forsook Egypt.

By faith "he" endured.

By faith "he" kept the Passover.

Yet even in this account of a great *individual leader*, we discover the *corporate dynamic* in Hebrews 11:29—by faith "*they*" passed through the Red Sea!

First it was "by faith *he*"...then it was "by faith *they*"....

In our day, we have left the enemy's territory, having been brought "out of darkness into His marvellous light" (1 Pet. 2:9). Satan and his demons, typified by Pharaoh and his army, have pursued us to the Red Sea that separates us from our destiny. Our backs are to the wall. There is no place to turn. There is only one way out....

As the end-time Church moves forward into the next century, we will face many obstacles. In the next few years, you and I are going to confront some unprecedented giants. The anointing upon each of us is powerful, and it *appears* that we are about to taste Pharaoh's wrath. Our only hope and confidence is to be a vital part of the "they." We will cross over because of our *corporate faith*, not merely because of anyone's individual faith.

According to *Webster's New Universal Unabridged Dictionary*[1], the English word "corporate" was derived from the Latin word *corpus*, which means "body." It defines "corporate" to mean:

1. United; combined.

2. United, in a legal body, as a number of individuals who are empowered to transact business as an individual; formed into a corporation; incorporated; as, a corporate town.

3. Belonging or pertaining to a corporation; as, corporate interests.

4. Shared by all members of a unified group; common; joint; as, corporate responsibility.

Our mind-sets must be transformed from a primarily individual viewpoint to a corporate way of life and thought. Both Testaments reveal the highest anointing to be corporate—it is the plural, compounded, collective anointing upon a *people*. God wants to anoint His whole family, His Church, the Body of Christ.

I am not speaking against individual anointing; rather, I am speaking for the neglected importance of *corporate anointing*. We are all joined to the Head and each other. The present-day emphasis of God's voice and Spirit is simple: "It's the whole Body or nobody."[2]

I believe that Jesus will literally return to this planet, although the much-anticipated "rapture" hasn't happened yet. However, regardless of our respective eschatologies, all of us remain postured on the threshold of a new day.

Many great men and women have emerged who carry the presence of God, and that is good. *But the Father still longs for a "holy nation"* (1 Pet. 2:9). The six chapters of the Book of Ephesians reveal this many-membered Man respectively to be *His Church*, *His Temple*, *His Family*, *His Body*, *His Bride*, and *His Army*—each exemplifying the corporate anointing. The anointing upon all of us is far greater than the anointing upon any one of us. By God's divine design, "the whole is greater than the sum of our parts."

I share the apostolic mandate of Paul, travailing like a woman in the pangs of labor until Christ is formed in a people. Whenever God commissions my tongue and hand to pen a new book, "I am again in the pains of childbirth" (Gal. 4:19 NIV). The purpose of this writing is to birth this apostolic burden in you. Like Joseph of Arimathaea, I am "begging" for the body of Jesus (Mt. 27:58)!

You are a principal spice, a vital ingredient, a necessary part of the new thing that God is manifesting in the earth. You have been apprehended by the King of glory to participate in the corporate anointing—Christ in the fullness of His Body!

This song from the Lord flowed through me one Sunday morning as I declared to my local church the truths about corporate anointing:

A new beginning
By His Spirit,
Fresh anointing
Upon each one,
Compound anointing
With His enabling,
From the Father
Through a corporate Son!

Pastor Kelley Varner
Praise Tabernacle
Richlands, North Carolina

Chapter One

The Anointing Is a Person

"…God hath sent forth *the Spirit of His Son*…."
Galatians 4:6

Anointing…

Everyone is talking about the anointing.

"We need the anointing."

"What a powerful anointing!"

"I want my ministry to be anointed."

These words are buzzing among the people of God. But what are we talking about?

The word "anointing" immediately evokes the thought of some great man or woman who lives and moves in the power of the Holy Spirit, one who manifests the power of God—some great *individual*, past or present, who was or is mightily anointed.

The Bible and Church history are filled with incredible stories of men and women who have been anointed in the name of the Lord. Thank God for personal anointing. I am anointed to write. You are anointed, enabled, and gifted by the grace of God to do what He has placed you in the earth to do.

We have begun to understand personal anointing and destiny. But now we must also consider *corporate anointing* and destiny.

Our mind-sets must be transformed from a primarily individual viewpoint to a corporate way of life and thought. Both Testaments reveal the highest anointing to be corporate—it is the plural, compounded, collective anointing upon a *people*. God wants to anoint His whole family, His Church, the Body of Christ.

The anointing is not a feeling, an idea, or an atmosphere. It is a knowing. It is the assurance that God is with us. And there is more…

The anointing is a Person—Immanuel, God with us; the Messiah, the Christ!

The Old Testament prophesied the coming of the "Messiah," and the New Testament faithfully records the fulfillment of those prophecies with the birth and ministry of the "Christ." This word was transliterated from the Greek word *christos*, which like its Hebrew equivalent, *Messiah*, means "the anointed one." Those are wonderful facts to know, but why is all this important to us today?

It is important because the dispensation of the fullness of times has dawned! The day of restoration and worldwide revival has come. Now is the time in which the Father predetermined that He would bring all things in Heaven and on earth together under one Head, even Christ.[1] The only way that will happen is through the anointing of Almighty God because our best efforts over the past years since Pentecost

have produced a weak and tasteless mixture of fleshly com-
promise, bickering, and only a little holiness.

The fountainhead of all anointing is the Lord Jesus
Christ, the Root of David, Earth's one true Messiah. All
truth, by precept and practice, must be founded upon the
centrality and supremacy of Jesus Christ, the everlastingly
preeminent One. That is why it is important to understand
that the anointing is not a thing but a *Person*.

The Anointing Comes Only
Through *the Anointed One*

In the Old Testament, prophets, priests, and kings were
anointed or consecrated with oil to set them apart unto their
offices of authority and leadership.[2]

Jesus, however, was and is *the* Messiah, the Christ, the
very Anointing of God. He is *the Prophet*, *the Priest*, and
the King.[3] Yet the New Testament also reveals that "Christ"
is even more: He is both *Head* and *Body*! Again you may be
asking the question, "Why is this important?"

Jesus is our glorious *Head* and we are His earthly *Body*,
the Church of Jesus Christ—the *corporate Messiah*! This
anointed, sanctified "royal priesthood" is a prophetic people
who have been made kings and priests unto God.[4] The
threefold anointing of prophet, priest, and king that abides
upon and within us all is the *corporate anointing*.

Christ	**produces**	**the Kingdom**
(Col. 1:27)		(Rom. 14:17)
The prophet	produces	righteousness.
The priest	produces	peace.
The king	produces	joy.

The Holy Spirit Is a Person

Jesus Christ is the "Anointed One," but His anointing flows like a river from Him who is our Head down to His earthly Body through the Holy Spirit. The Holy Spirit is *the Spirit of the Son* described by Paul in Galatians 4:6. The Spirit of the Son is therefore also the "Anointed One."

Once you understand that the Holy Spirit is also a Person sent from the Father and represents the Son, you will better understand why the Bible does not refer to Him as an "it," but rather uses the pronouns of Deity.[5]

God in the Person of the Holy Spirit, the Spirit of the Son...

1. Teaches (Jn. 14:26).

2. Testifies (Jn. 15:26).

3. Reproves (Jn. 16:8-11).

4. Guides into truth (Jn. 16:13).

5. Speaks (Acts 13:2).

6. Calls men into service (Acts 13:2).

7. Directs men in service (Acts 16:6-7).

8. Prays and intercedes for us (Rom. 8:26-27).

9. Searches all things, even the deep things of God (1 Cor. 2:10).

10. Works through us (1 Cor. 12:11).

The Person of the Holy Spirit can be...

1. Blasphemed (Mt. 12:31-32).

2. Lied to (Acts 5:3).

3. Tempted or tested (Acts 5:9).

4. Resisted (Acts 7:51).

5. Grieved (Eph. 4:30).

6. Insulted (Heb. 10:29).

It is important for us to rearrange our thinking to conform to God's mind, as revealed in His Word. I've listed all these attributes of the Holy Spirit to make it clear that our actions (or lack of them) toward Him do play a part in our success or failure in God's Kingdom. To understand the corporate anointing, we must understand that the Holy Spirit is God's anointing abiding in His earthly temples. This Person is the Spirit of the Father and the Son who together have come to make the *saints* their "mansion" or "abode."[6] For this reason, our bodies are called the "temple" of the Holy Ghost.[7]

Bear with me when I repeat this important point: *The anointing is a Person* (not a thing). "For in Him [not 'it'] we live, and move, and have our being" (Acts 17:28a). The wonder of this new creation reality abiding in the hearts of believers is described by the apostle Paul as "Christ in you" (Col. 1:27). Now let me blend these thoughts about Jesus the Christ and the *christos* or "anointing" of the Holy Spirit by noting two primary truths about the Christ, the Anointed One of God:

1. Christ is more than an individual.

2. Christ never left the planet.

"Christ" is more than an individual. The apostle Paul unfolded this Messianic mystery in his Epistle to the Colossians.

Col. 1:25-27, NIV

I have become its servant by the commission God gave me to present to you the word of God in its fullness—

the mystery that has been kept hidden for ages and generations, but is now disclosed to the saints.

*To them God has chosen to make known among the Gentiles the glorious riches of this mystery, which is **Christ in you**, the hope of glory.*

1 Tim. 3:16, NIV

*Beyond all question, the mystery of godliness is great: **He appeared in a body**....*

Christ in and Among All of You

The word "you" in Colossians 1:27 is a *plural* pronoun. Why is this important? The *highest* anointing is the *corporate anointing*, and the mystery of godliness is best summed up in the properly translated foundational phrase, "Christ in and among **all of you**."

Some see Jesus Christ the Head, but have never discerned the Lord's Body.[8] They have yet to experience the Holy Ghost in the Pentecostal dynamic, to speak with other tongues and discover the supernatural gifts of the Spirit.

Men have confined apostles and prophets and the *charismata* or grace gifts of the Spirit to the "past history" of the Book of Acts.[9] They have failed to understand that in God's economy, these things happened only *the day before yesterday!*[10] Calvary predicated or laid the groundwork for Pentecost: First came the blood of redemption, then the oil of anointing and consecration. My dear brethren among the "staunch evangelicals" need to be introduced to the mystery of "Christ in you"; they need to see the Body of Christ *by the Spirit* manifesting all the *fullness* of Christ instead of the limitations of man.

Others have tended to emphasize the mystery of Christ in His aggregate Body while failing to "hold fast" or maintain their connection to the Head, even doing away with Jesus' literal return to this planet.[11] Their basic weakness is that they have made the emphasis of their sonship *singular* or earthbound. They worship the process rather than the One who does the transformation.

Both views are necessary—the *Anointed One* of the New Testament is revealed in both Jesus the Head and His Body the Church.[12]

I am not "Christ." You are not "Christ." Christ as He is revealed in the earth is not an individual. Why? In His fullest expression, *Christ is plural.* His Church, His Body, collectively comprises the fullness of Christ in the earth. Paul said it best in his letter to the Ephesians:

Eph. 1:22-23, NIV

> *And God placed all things under His feet and appointed Him to be head over everything for the church,*
>
> *which is His body, the fullness of Him who fills everything in every way.*

For that to happen corporately, Christ must first be experienced personally. Paul reiterated this new creation reality to the Galatians and the Ephesians.

Gal. 4:6, NIV

> *Because you are sons, God sent **the Spirit of His Son** into our hearts, the Spirit who calls out, "Abba, Father."*

Eph. 5:18, KJV

> *...be filled with the Spirit.*

Christ in you...the Spirit of the Son sent into our hearts...being filled with the Holy Ghost—all these spiritual synonyms express the same truth concerning God's anointing. The Persons of the Son and the Spirit are distinct and yet so closely intertwined that they defy separation.

Paul defined "Christ" as "the image of God" to the Corinthians.[13] The image of God, which is our future and destiny, is held within the Messianic seed! The ultimate goal of Jesus' present reign is to see the Father's ultimate intention and expectation birthed in the earth: *to raise up a vast family of sons and daughters* conformed to the image of the Firstborn, a corporate expression of Jesus' life and nature.[14]

To accomplish this, the Father *sent forth the Spirit of His Son* into our hearts. Just as the spirit of Moses the Old Testament mediator was multiplied and placed upon the 70 elders, so the New Testament Mediator has become a many-membered Man in His corporate Body![15]

The mystery of this New Testament revelation began with a Seed being planted in a habitation of purity, Mary's virgin womb. Paul's apostolic, intercessory burden was that Christ, the Anointed One in the Spirit of the Son, be fully formed in a virgin Church![16] This glorious Body of Christ is the Church of the firstborn, Mount Zion, the city of the living God.[17] Paul had firsthand knowledge of the reality of the indwelling Christ. He wrote to the Galatians:

Gal 1:15-16, KJV

> *But when it pleased God, who separated me from my mother's womb, and called me by His grace,*
>
> *To reveal His Son in me, that I might preach Him....*

Now it is our turn. It's time for the Messiah to appear, for Christ to come. It's time for the Head of the Church to manifest Himself, to unveil Himself, to form Himself *in us* as a separated people, as His Body—*the unified, many-membered Messiah on earth* endued from on high with corporate anointing.

"Christ" Never Left the Planet

Christ is more than an individual. The Father, through the outpouring of the Holy Ghost (the Spirit of the Son), has multiplied His Son Jesus into a many-membered Man. For this reason, I can declare with absolute confidence that "Christ" never left the planet! Consider the spiritual precedent of Elijah and Elisha in the Book of Second Kings.

2 Kings 2:8-14, KJV

> *And Elijah took his **mantle**, and wrapped it together, and smote the waters, and they were divided hither and thither, so that they two went over on dry ground.*
>
> *And it came to pass, when they were gone over, that Elijah said unto Elisha, Ask what I shall do for thee, before I be taken away from thee. And Elisha said, I pray thee, **let a double portion of thy spirit be upon me**.*
>
> *And he said, **Thou hast asked a hard thing**: nevertheless, **if thou see me** when I am taken from thee, it shall be so unto thee; but if not, it shall not be so.*
>
> *...and Elijah went up by a whirlwind into heaven.*
>
> *And Elisha saw it...and he took hold of his own clothes, and rent them in two pieces.*
>
> *He took up also the mantle of Elijah that fell from him, and went back, and stood by the bank of Jordan;*
>
> *And **he took the mantle of Elijah that fell from him, and smote the waters, and said, Where is the Lord God of Elijah?**...*

Elijah went up, but his *mantle* came down. Elijah ascended, but *the mentor's anointing* remained in the earth to rest upon his spiritual son. The parallel is obvious: Jesus went up, but *His Spirit* came down. Jesus ascended, but "Christ," the anointing (*christos*) of the *Anointed One*, remained in the earth to rest upon His Church.

The Hebrew word for "mantle" in this passage is the feminine form of *'addiyrr*, which means "something ample; wide, large; figuratively, powerful."[18] It is also translated as "excellent, famous, gallant, glorious, goodly, lordly, mighty, noble, principal, worthy" in the King James Version. The reason I've quoted so many adjectives is simple: *They literally describe the collective anointing that rests upon Jesus and His Church.* The root word for "mantle" means "to expand, be great or magnificent." This "double portion," literally, "the portion of the firstborn," belongs to all of us who are heirs of God and joint-heirs with Christ![19]

Where Is the Lord God of Elijah?

The only criterion for receiving Elijah's anointing was that Elisha "see" him as he was taken up in ascension. Too many Christians only see the Lord Jesus in His crucifixion. They need to discover the resurrected Lord who *ascended*, the greatest Son of David now exalted and enthroned far above all things. We must see Him as He is, not just as He was.

When Elijah ascended into Heaven by a whirlwind, Elisha the younger prophet "took" or "raised up" the mantle of his spiritual father after Elijah's mantle "fell" from him.[20] Centuries later, Elijah's spirit also rested upon John the Baptist.[21] In an even greater day, when Jesus the Son of God was raised up to the right hand of the Father, the Holy Spirit of Jesus "fell" upon the early Church.[22] The Greek word for "fell" is *epipipto*, and it means "to embrace with affection."[23] The love of God has been poured out into our hearts by the Holy Ghost, and the Lord God of Elijah literally dwells in the corporate Body of His Son today![24]

The end-time Church is "amphitheatered" about or sur-
rounded by those who died in Christ by faith long before
His first coming.[25] Although they are not complete apart
from us, their anointed way of life—their spoken and written words, and especially the laying on of their hands—and
their spirits live on. They are not dead. When we think of
them or recall their feats of faith and prophetic anointing,
they are instantly right here with us. Even the memory of
them is anointed.

"Christ," their collective *christos* or anointing, never left
the planet. It did more than simply fall to the ground. It is
multiplying and compounding itself exponentially! Like the
rising waters of the river in Ezekiel's prophetic vision, this
generational, corporate anointing has steadily risen to the
ankles, knees, and loins. Now we have finally come to that
epochal span when there are waters to swim in, a river that
cannot be passed over.[26]

We know from Peter's Epistles that "...one day is with
the Lord as a thousand years, and a thousand years as one
day" (2 Pet 3:8). In the realm of the prophetic, even distances
can take on eternal meanings and significance. Each time the
waters were measured in Ezekiel's vision, the distance was
1,000 cubits (or 1,500 feet). The total span of the "waters to
swim in" was 4,000 cubits or 6,000 feet (Ezek. 47:3-5). In
biblical chronology, the purposes of God have brought us
6,000 years or "six days" from Adam, and at the same time,
2,000 years or "two days" from the earthly ministry of Jesus
Christ. We are living in the *dawning of the seventh day* from
Adam and *the third day* from Jesus![27]

Every great advance of God's corporate people is pre-
ceded by warfare. The twentieth century marks a stretch of
unprecedented spiritual warfare. Moses and Aaron had to
confront the magicians of Egypt before Pharaoh would let

God's people go.[28] The prophet Elijah had to challenge the false prophets of Baal to move the Israelites into the *corporate action* of rounding up the false prophets for destruction.[29] The apostles Peter and Paul resisted the demon-inspired sorcerers Simon and Barjesus (Elymas) when they hindered the apostles' declaration and demonstration of the gospel.[30]

In this day, the corporate, generational anointing upon the corporate Son, the end-time Body of Christ, has begun to confront head-on the collective, supernatural powers of darkness as well!

This anointing is a Person—the Holy Ghost, the Spirit of the Son. Jesus, the divine Seed, fell into the ground and died.[31] He has come forth in glorious resurrection and is now enthroned in unparalleled majesty and splendor. From that kingly posture He has poured out His own Spirit upon the nations of the earth.[32] As with the woman in the days of Elisha, the oil of anointing has multiplied, and the anointing upon the Head has flowed down to His Body—the *corporate anointing*![33] The apostle John saw this corporate Man in the midst of seven golden candlesticks, having a voice as the sound of many waters.[34]

1 Cor. 12:12, KJV

> *For as the body is one, and hath many members, and all the members of that one body, being many, are one body: so also is* [the] *Christ.*

In America, men have substituted talent for anointing, but the anointing is still a Person. As we continue to define the anointing by examining the Hebrew and Greek words of the Old and New Testaments, we will soon realize that the corporate anointing is revealed in *three dimensions....*

Chapter Two

Corporate Anointing in Three Dimensions

"Have not I written to thee *excellent*
[triple, threefold] things…?"

Proverbs 22:20

You have already learned that the anointing is a Person, and that God the Father "…sent forth the Spirit of His Son into [our] hearts" after Jesus' ascension (Gal. 4:6). But did you know that the original Hebrew and Greek terms of the Old and New Testament respectively demonstrate *three dimensions* to the anointing? All three dimensions are pictured and paralleled by the three anointings in the life of King David, the man after God's own heart.

Threefold Things

God's three greatest spokesmen—Moses, Jesus, and Paul—all declared that by the mouth of two or three witnesses all things would be confirmed and established.[1]

Prov. 22:20-21, KJV

*Have not I written to thee **excellent things** in counsels and knowledge,*

That I might make thee know the certainty of the words of truth...?

God's purposes are revealed throughout the Scriptures in three dimensions. The word for "excellent things" here is *shaylish* and means "a triple, (as a musical instrument) a triangle (or perhaps rather three-stringed lute); also a threefold measure; also (as an officer) a general of the third rank (upward, the highest)." This word can also indicate "weighty" things.[2]

To live is to grow. To grow is to change. And spiritual growth denotes change after change after change.[3] We learn the things of God "precept upon precept" and "line upon line" (Is. 28:10).

These "excellent" or "threefold" things signify not only that there are three levels, so that one is preferred above another, but also that three parts are required to make a whole. Each ingredient is equally needed to fill its place. When any portion is lacking, there are limitations, making the overall vision incomplete.

One does not discard the first or second realm when moving on into the third. Instead, the lesser dimensions are swallowed up in the greater, for the "in part" is contained in the whole. For example, Israel was commanded to keep all three feasts.[4] Jesus Christ is "altogether lovely," our Savior, Baptizer, and King (Song 5:16).

The foundational study for "threefold things" is the Tabernacle of Moses, built according to the divine "pattern" (Ex. 25:40)—the Outer Court, the Holy Place, and the Most Holy Place.[5] Consider these examples of "threefold" things:

Outer Court	Holy Place	Most Holy Place
For all Israel	For the priests	For the high priest
Feast of Passover	Pentecost	Tabernacles
Out of Egypt	Through the wilderness	Into the land
Jesus (Savior)	Christ (anointing)	The Lord
Born-again	Spirit-filled	Mature
30-fold	60-fold	100-fold
Thanksgiving	Praise	Worship
All man	God and man	All God
External	Internal	Eternal
The Way	The Truth	The Life
Faith	Hope	Love
First anointing	Second anointing	Third anointing
Poured out	Smeared on	Rubbed in

The last example of threefold things shows the essence of the Hebrew and Greek words for "anointing." Corporate anointing is three-dimensional, revealed in the different words for "anointing" or "anointed."

The first is the Hebrew word *sûk*, which means to "pour out."

The second is the Hebrew word *mašah* or *mashach*, which means to "smear on."

The third is the Greek word *chrio*, which means to "rub in."

The First Scent and Beginning of God's Anointing

Each dimension of the anointing reveals ever-increasing levels of divine power according to God's Word. Yet each dimension of the anointing has a specific purpose in the plan of God, and at each level we encounter not a "thing" but a Person, the Spirit of the Son of God.

Is. 10:27, KJV

> And it shall come to pass in **that day**, that [the Assyrian] burden shall be taken away from off thy shoulder, and his yoke from off thy neck, and the yoke shall be destroyed because of the **anointing**.

Church leaders have traditionally defined the "anointing" as the "burden-removing, yoke-destroying power of God" in accordance with this Scripture passage from the Book of Isaiah. But what has not been so common is the understanding that "that day" is now *this day*. Yes, this is the New Testament day. The word for "burden" means "load" and comes from a root word meaning "to carry." This "yoke" is imposed upon the neck and shoulders and is a symbol for the will (it is rendered as "slave-yoke" in The Living Bible). Isaiah the prophet assured us that the enemy's bondages would be destroyed because of the anointing. Since this "burden-removing, yoke-destroying" Person has been sent to our hearts in *this day*, then we need to learn how to receive Him fully.

The first dimension of the corporate anointing is revealed in the Hebrew root *cuwk* or *sûk*, which means "to smear over (with oil), anoint."[6] According to *The Theological Wordbook of the Old Testament*, *sûk* primarily means *"pour*, in anointing."

As a pouring, it [*sûk*] differs from its most common synonym *mašah* which includes the idea of "spreading" or "smearing"...*Sûk* may be used of the ordinary physical process of anointing the body with olive oil, particularly after bathing (2 Sam. 12:20), for especially fragrant effect (Ruth 3:3). It was often used for medicinal needs (Ezek. 16:9; cf. Lk. 10:34)...[and was] a symbol of gladness... (2 Chron. 28:15).[7]

When the anointing oil was *poured out* upon an individual in an Old Testament ceremony, it ran down over the surfaces of the body and excited the senses, but quickly dissipated.

The first phase of compound anointing is a momentary fragrance, a perfume. It is a fleeting feeling and glory, soon evaporating as its fragrance dwindles. There is nothing wrong with this beginning kind of anointing; the problem is that it doesn't go deep enough into the life. Interestingly, *sûk* is found in only eight verses of the Old Testament, and eight is the biblical number denoting resurrection or a new beginning!

The Holy Ghost is the Spirit that raised Jesus from the dead.[8] The anointing—the Spirit of the Son—is the very embodiment of divine energy, the Spirit of the Son *sent* with purpose and responsibility. We have responded to the presence of God with exuberance, but too often we don't allow the anointing to permeate our very being.

It is all right to have a good time in the house of the Lord, but how often do we find that when the next day's testings come, we do not have enough of the Spirit's enrichment left to face our trials in triumph?

Those who remain in this first realm ask everyone to pray that they will "hold out to the end." Theirs is an endurance contest. They are always "waiting for the next meeting," hoping that somehow the Spirit will be poured out upon them again. An intermittent "touch" from God is all they want.

The Second Taste: Get *Smeared* With God

The second level of corporate anointing is seen in the Hebrew root *mashach*, which means "to rub with oil, to anoint; by implication, to consecrate; also to paint."[9] In other words, it means to *smear on*.

The Theological Wordbook of the Old Testament adds that *mashach* can also mean "to spread a liquid."[10] *Mashach* is especially used (over 25 times) in Exodus, Leviticus, and Numbers concerning the Levitical economy and the Aaronic priesthood.[11] Found frequently in the historical books with regard to anointing kings,[12] *mashach* is used only twice in the prophets.[13] The first level of corporate anointing won't keep you. You must stand still long enough for Him to *smear it on*.

The noun, *mashiyach*, is derived from *mashach*, and it usually refers to a consecrated person (as a king, priest, or saint); specifically, the Messiah.[14] It occurs about 40 times, primarily in First and Second Samuel and the Book of Psalms.[15]

When the anointing oil was smeared on, it lasted longer than when it was just poured out. We have rejoiced because the anointings of the Spirit worked through us, and certain victories were obtained, yet these experiences were still "in part." Like the priests of old, we have been anointed for service, but there are still limitations in this second realm.

These Old Testament words only take us through two of the three dimensions of the corporate anointing. The New Testament gives us two additional words for "anointing": *aleipho* and *chrio*.

Aleipho seems to pick up the meanings of *sûk* and *mashach*—to pour out and to smear on—carrying them over into the New Testament. It means "to oil (with perfume)."[16] However, it is the final Greek word, *chrio*, that takes us further into our destiny as the Body of Christ.

The Third Dimension:
When God Is *Rubbed* Into Our Very Being

Lk. 4:18, KJV

The Spirit of the Lord is upon Me, because He hath anointed Me to preach the gospel to the poor....

The Greek word *chrio*, translated as "anointed" in this verse, gives us the scope of the third dimension of corporate anointing—to *rub in*. According to Strong's, it means "through the idea of contact, to smear on or rub with oil, (by implication) to consecrate to an office or religious service."[17] *Chrio* is more limited in its use than *aleipho* because it is nearly always reserved for the sacred anointings of the Lord Jesus Christ as the "anointed" of God.[18] Only once does *chrio* allude to believers.[19] In the Septuagint (the Greek translation of the Old Testament from Hebrew and Aramaic), *chrio* was used by the translators with regard to priests, kings, and prophets.[20]

While *chrio* is the Greek verb or "action word" for anointing, the Greek noun is *chrisma*. It means "an unguent or smearing, (figuratively) the special endowment of the Holy Spirit."[21] It is found but three times, translated in the King James Version once as "unction" (1 Jn. 2:20) and twice as "anointing" (1 Jn. 2:27).

This third dimension of the corporate anointing is the one that abides and proves to be our complete sufficiency. The anointing that rested upon the Lord Jesus was the *Chrisma*, the Spirit *without measure*.[22] This is the fullness we desire: *an unlimited supply that abides,* permeating every fiber of our being. This third anointing pertains to the Most Holy Place, where all compound anointing springs forth from the finished work of Jesus Christ.

This third anointing, the one without measure, is described in the Book of Revelation as "the seven Spirits of God" (Rev. 3:1).[23] The number seven denotes completeness or fullness. The prophet Isaiah names these seven aspects of the full Messianic anointing that would rest upon Jesus and His Church, the extension of His life and ministry.

Is. 11:1-2, KJV

And there shall come forth a rod [Jesus] *out of the stem* [David] *of Jesse, and a Branch* [the Church] *shall grow out of his roots:*

And the spirit of the Lord shall rest upon Him [both Head and Body], *the spirit of wisdom and understanding, the spirit of counsel and might, the spirit of knowledge and of the fear of the Lord.*

Jn. 15:5, KJV

I am the vine, ye are the branches....

The Maturing Pressure of God's "Hand"

This final anointing is rubbed in *by the pressure of God's hand.* The "hand" ministry, the fivefold ascension gift ministries mentioned in Ephesians 4:11, is the means by which the Lord has determined to mature His Church. The thumb represents the apostle, covering and touching all four fingers in intimate co-labor. The index finger is the prophet, the pointer. The middle finger extends or reaches out the fartherest to grasp the lost, a picture of the evangelist. The pastor, married to the local church, is depicted by the ring finger of the marriage covenant. And the teacher is the little finger, the only one that can get into your ear!

Just before Jesus surrendered Himself as the sacrificed Lamb for the Passover slaughter, He took His disciples to the garden of Gethsemane and said, "What, could ye not watch with Me one hour?" (Mt. 26:40b)

"Gethsemane" means "olive-press." Only those who have been pressed and pressured by the "hand" of God—His government and divine order—will participate in the third anointing. A genuine apostle or prophet will not tell God's children what they want to hear, but rather, like a good parent, what they *need* to hear. A real man or woman of God will rub you the right way—toward God. The Word of the Kingdom will put pressure on you.[24] But stay with it. Stay with the pastor, the set man (the one God "set" into the place of leadership by His own counsel, not by the opinions of man). Stay with the vision. You will become a vital part of a glorious Church that will be anointed three times—you will see God's presence and glory poured out, smeared on, and rubbed in!

What does this third anointing look like after it is rubbed in? You can't see it, but it's there! Those who are called to walk in all three levels of corporate anointing are not strutting their flesh. They have refused the fast lane that ambitiously seeks the glory of men. Their lives or ministries may not look like much, visibly speaking, to those caught up in the game of counting nickels and noses. But if you get close to a person who has allowed the anointing to be *rubbed in*, your spiritual sense of smell will discern his or her "savor" and discern the life-giving "fragrance and scent" of *His* life.[25] At this stage, the fullness of Christ dwells in the heart by faith.[26]

Little children delight in the *first dimension* of the anointing. As the refreshing of the Spirit is poured out, it flows over them, titillating their senses, and they feel good. *Spiritual adolescents* seek for more—and find that the anointing will empower them for limited service—yet they cling to this *second realm*. But there are those *mature ones* who earnestly desire the full in-working of the Spirit found only in the *third dimension* of the corporate anointing. They are determined to pursue Him, regardless of how severe the process of death to self is, in order that Christ alone be seen in them.

David's Three Anointings

As I mentioned earlier, the threefold anointing of God is clearly pictured in the life of King David, whom God declared was "a man after Mine own heart, which shall fulfil all My will" (Acts 13:22).

First Anointing	Second Anointing	Third Anointing
(1 Sam. 16:13)	(2 Sam. 2:4)	(2 Sam. 5:3)
sûk	*mashach*	*chrio/chrisma*
Poured out	Smeared on	Rubbed in
Exalted son	King over praise	Lord of all
Killed a bear, lion, and giant	Ruled the tribe of Judah	King over all of Israel

The First Anointing Is Poured Out

1 Sam. 16:13, KJV

*Then Samuel took the horn of oil, and **anointed** him in the midst of his brethren: and the Spirit of the Lord came upon David from that day forward....*

Samuel *poured out* a horn of oil upon Saul's successor. Even as the prophet pointed to David as God's anointed, the eternal purpose of the Holy Spirit was to reveal Jesus the Son, *the Anointed*. David's seven brothers were rejected by the Lord because they resembled Saul;[27] they were "head and shoulders" men (picturing human wisdom and human strength). David was the eighth son of Jesse. A type of King Jesus, this sweet psalmist of Israel was the exalted son anointed in the house of the father in the midst of the brethren.[28] David's gradual ascent into Zion prefigures our Lord's ascension, exaltation, and coronation at the right hand of the Father.

This first anointing was but the beginning of David's journey, and with that initial enabling he killed a bear, a lion, and the uncircumcised giant Goliath. The weight of that first oil poured out upon his ruddy head was greater than the crown he would eventually wear. It was good, but it did not immediately place him upon the throne. It led him into uncharted territory—the preparation process, with all its training and discipline.

David desperately needed that fundamental anointing to face the wilderness experiences that lay before him. Those early times of testing are not easy to take, but thank God He anoints us for them. Even Jesus the Pattern Son faced the threefold trial of the lust of the flesh, the lust of the eyes, and the pride of life.[29] Yet if we yield to the in-working of the Holy Spirit, He will guide us.[30] We will do well to conserve His inflow, for it is the divine energy of God that brings us through His dealings.

The Second Anointing Is Smeared On

2 Sam. 2:4, KJV

And the men of Judah came, and there they **anointed** [*mashach*] *David king over the house of Judah....*

2 Sam 3:39, KJV

And I am this day weak, though **anointed** [*mashach*] *king....*

David's second anointing was *smeared on* by the tribe of Judah in Hebron. He began to reign as king, but it was an administration limited to "Judah," which means "praise." When God anoints His people to praise Him, we experience the oil of joy and exchange the garment of praise for the spirit of heaviness.[31] This brings certain victories, but reigning in praise is not totally sufficient. Once we thought everything was done by prayer, so we prayed loud and long.

Then we learned fasting, and much was accomplished as we set ourselves to seek the Lord. Then new horizons opened up through hours of worshiping the Lord, and we learned how to rule through the power of praise. But, like David, we discovered that although we have been made kings and priests through Christ,[32] we were still "weak" or "fainthearted" (Deut. 20:8). Now we must add to our faith.[33] We still pray, fast, and praise, but now we press into a greater land of promise, a third realm of corporate anointing beyond Pentecost.

The Third and Highest Anointing Is Rubbed In

2 Sam. 3:1, KJV

Now there was long war between the house of Saul and the house of David: but David waxed stronger and stronger, and the house of Saul waxed weaker and weaker.

2 Sam. 5:3, KJV

*So **all the elders of Israel** came to the king to Hebron; and king David made a league with them in Hebron before the Lord: and **they anointed** David king over Israel.*

This is an Old Testament picture of the New Testament reality of *chrio*, the corporate "rubbed in" anointing of God. Although the word *mashach* is used here for "anointed," the third level of anointing is revealed here because *all of Israel rubbed in* this third anointing, and David took complete dominion over all things as the uniting king of both Israel and Judah. Just prior to that, there was "long war" between the house of Saul (the mind of the flesh) and the house of David (the mind of the Spirit).

There's a whole lot of David and a little bit of Saul in all of us—these two men reside between our ears. The more the Christ-life is rubbed in, the greater will be the war waged with any remaining part of *self*.

In truth, the war is over; it is finished.[34] The problem is that we have yet to appropriate His complete victory. This good fight of faith seems to be long, but we are receiving an anointing that remains, and Christ in us shall prevail. When this third anointing has completely transformed every part, we will know the blessedness of the *full dominion* of the Spirit over the flesh.[35]

The "Saul" that was in David—his own individual ideas and opinions—had to die. Jehovah didn't need another madman on the throne. Personal agendas are swallowed up by corporate anointing.

David, as a type of King Jesus, made a "league" or "covenant" with the people of God in "Hebron," a city whose very name means "to join," signifying union and fellowship. This third level of *corporate anointing* requires a great commitment. Those who are joined to the Lord become one with His heart and spirit.[36] The Church has been predestined to be fully anointed the same way Jesus was anointed. We as one people must allow the "hand" of God to rub in the holy ointment until we have been transfigured into Messiah's "same image" (2 Cor. 3:18). We are anointed because we are related to the Anointed One.

The mainstream of the Spirit-filled Body of Christ is postured somewhere between the second and third anointings. We have ruled through praise but have yet to take our rightful place of full dominion. Between the "smearing on" and the "rubbing in," between the Feasts of Pentecost and Tabernacles, there is a "long war" (2 Sam. 3:1), and a long walk of patience and endurance. The more you go on to know the Lord, the more you will face resistance. Few are willing to pay the price it takes to walk the narrow way into this high calling.[37] Are you willing to answer His call to the narrow way of the rubbed-in anointing?

Be like a thermostat, not a thermometer. Refuse to go up and down according to the surrounding spiritual climate. Grow beyond the immature satisfaction of having just a "touch" from the Lord. The third dimension of corporate anointing *abides*. It doesn't pour out and roll off. When you have this anointing, this Person the Bible calls "the Spirit of the Son," rubbed in, He becomes you, and you become Him.

In his ultimate anointing, David became lord over all. He took dominion as God originally intended man to do from the beginning.[38] Whether you are a man or a woman, once you have the oil of God rubbed in, you will walk and live in the anointing, carrying the very presence of the Lord!

How did God anoint Jesus of Nazareth?[39] Jesus was born of the Spirit, baptized in water, and filled with the Holy Ghost.[40] He was then "led" by that same Spirit into the wilderness (like David) to be tested (Lk. 4:1-14).[41] But then He returned to His hometown in the *dunamis* "power and ability" of the Spirit, stood up in His home church, opened the Word, and declared, "The Spirit of the Lord is upon Me, because He has *rubbed it in*!" (Lk. 4:18)

The first and second anointings, the ointment poured out and smeared on, will only meet our own needs, heal our own bodies, and pay our own bills. But what do we have left for the nations? God wants to *rub in the third anointing* so that we can carry His presence into all the earth.[42] Then each of us will be able to pour out and smear His glory on others. Furthermore, real brethren who are bone of bone and flesh of flesh will get close enough to each other until the fullness of the anointing is mutually rubbed in and mingled, producing the fullness of compounded anointing.

The scope of compounded anointing is vast, fully expressed only in three dimensions. Both Testaments abound with instructive examples of corporate anointing, beginning with the Book of Genesis.

Chapter Three

Scriptural Examples of Corporate Anointing

"...in the volume of the book it is written of Me...."

Hebrews 10:7

The Bible reveals many examples of the threefold *anointing*, the Spirit of the Son sent to our hearts. Once again, we must remember that the anointing is not an "it" or a thing; the anointing is a Person. As David was anointed three times, so the corporate anointing and glory of the New Testament —"Christ" Jesus the *Head* and the Church His *Body*—is unveiled in three dimensions.

That same anointing is pictured in the Old Testament as being *poured out* at the Feast of Passover, *smeared on* in the Feast of Pentecost, and *rubbed in* during the Feast of Tabernacles. The original Hebrew and Greek words of Scripture have defined the three dimensions of the anointing for us. Now we will go to the Book of Genesis, the divine "seed-plot" and birthing ground of virtually every holy precept and plan of God. Here we will uncover many examples that clarify and amplify the truth about corporate anointing.

Good and Very Good

The very first chapter of the Bible reveals a divine pattern and *a divine preference* that we should not ignore! Genesis chapter 1 describes the handiwork of Elohim, the Creator God, in the crescendo of creation.

Six times, one time at the end of each recorded day of creation, God uttered these words into the new realm of energy and matter He had made: "It is good." He said this with regard to the light, the sky and the seas, the dry ground and the herbs and trees reproducing themselves, the two great lights, the living things that filled the waters and the air, and the creatures of the earth.[1] Six times God said of each facet and component of creation, "It is good."

Gen. 1:31, KJV

*And God saw **every thing** that He had made, and, behold, it was **very good**....*

Here we see a divine pattern of blessing when the Creator of all said, "Good, good, good, good, good, good..." And then He said something in the seventh day that He longs to say again: "*Very good!*" It was only when God looked at *everything together* that He said it was "very" good! God reserves His highest pleasure and blessing for that which is whole and complete, with each of its good parts *joined together*.

As New Testament believers, you and I have been "born again" from above, and we are part of His *new creation*, created by and for His pleasure.[2] In Him, you are good and I am good.

Because of His enabling, your ministry is good and my ministry is good. Your church and your pastor are good—just as my church and my pastor are good. Individually and uniquely, each of us is good. As the saying goes, "the water tastes like the garden hose." God has arranged things so that each one of us has something to do that no else can do the way that we can, and we can celebrate that to a certain extent. Yet there is a place of greater truth and greater good revealed in the Book of Beginnings and echoed throughout God's Word.

Each personal aspect of the individual members of God's new creation is "good," but *together*, *corporately combined and mingled*, we are "very good," wholly good, exceedingly good.[3]

Altogether Lovely

Song 5:16, KJV

> *...yea, he is **altogether** lovely. This is my beloved, and this is my friend, O daughters of Jerusalem.*

The Song of Solomon is the "song of songs" (Song 1:1), and may be seen as a "song" for the Holy of Holies.[4] Jesus Christ, the great Bridegroom, is typified by King Solomon, the "beloved" of the Shulamite, who prefigures the Church, the Bride of Christ.

Inasmuch as Solomon and the Shulamite are wed in chapter 3, chapters 4 through 8 tell the story of *married love*. In Song of Solomon 5:10-16, the Shulamite bride intimately describes her husband from head to toe. Each of these ten facets are layered with truth that applies to our journey toward maturity and unity today:

1. Behold His head — His wisdom (Song 5:11).

2. Behold His locks — His vigor (Song 5:11).

3. Behold His eyes — His insight (Song 5:12).

4. Behold His cheeks — His flexibility (Song 5:13).

5. Behold His lips — His worship (Song 5:13).

6. Behold His hands — His service (Song 5:14).

7. Behold His belly — His motives (Song 5:14).

8. Behold His legs — His stability (Song 5:15).

9. Behold His countenance — His vision (Song 5:15).

10. Behold His mouth — His ministry (Song 5:16).

The Shulamite bride knew all about her kingly husband. She had experienced all of him. Each of these singular aspects is a rich study in Christology—the Person and work of Jesus Christ. (And they are also a picture of our corporate destiny as the Bride of Christ, knowing and experiencing all of our Christ, our risen King and Groom.)

God is love, and Jesus is the Son of God as well as God the Son. Each of these ten facets of His manifold grace and character are "lovely" or "delightful." But when *combined*, they are "altogether" lovely (Song 5:16)! This Hebrew word, *kole*, means "the whole...often in a plural sense." It is taken from a primitive root meaning "to complete," and is rendered in the King James Version as "(make) *perfect*" in Ezekiel 27:4,11.[5]

Why is all this important? Each of these ten perspectives of the Lord's total Person are sometimes "compartmentalized" into denominational or sectarian divisions by those with lesser vision. Why else would we have a "Baptist Jesus," a "Methodist Jesus," a "Pentecostal Jesus," a "Roman Catholic Jesus," or a "Kingdom Jesus"? The essential meaning of "integrity" is "wholeness." When any group sets forth its pet doctrine, or part of the truth as *the whole truth*, that group loses its integrity. Jesus is the Sum of all His delightful parts[6]—He is *altogether* lovely! Now He wants us to abandon every artificial wall of separation so we can exhibit His unity and loveliness on earth as it is in Heaven. His loveliness is manifested only when His people are *all together*!

He Becomes We

1 Jn. 4:17, KJV

> *Herein is our love made perfect, **that we may have boldness** in the day of judgment: because **as He is, so are we** in this world.*

As *He* is by nature, so are *we* by nature...

Jesus' Bride, the Church, has been called out of darkness to become a Companion of like nature and ability—not when we die and go to Heaven, but in *this "world."* We are too quick to dismiss His decreed destiny to cover this *cosmos*—this "temporary, cosmetic, melts-in-the-fire, transient system, order, and arrangement of things"—with His glory.[7] That is why He purposely left *His Body* behind when He ascended to the Father.

He becomes *we*!

This end-time, "third-day people"[8] will be given dominion in the earth by virtue of their having been conformed to His image and likeness.[9] According to John the apostle, our global ministry will be marked by "boldness." This is translated from the Greek word *parrhesia* used in First John 4:17. It means "all out-spokenness, frankness, bluntness, publicity; by implication, assurance."[10] Such is the dynamic ministry of the "new creation many-membered Man" who will go forth in corporate anointing!

Character cannot be imparted through the laying on of hands. The Christ nature (and character) is apostolically grown and built within a people as "He" becomes "we"!

The Servant of Servants

The Bible reveals Jesus Christ to be the King of kings, the Lord of lords, and the God of gods.[11]

In stark contrast, He is also the Servant of servants. Isaiah described the Messiah as the "servant" of Jehovah (Is. 42:1-5). This takes on critical importance when we understand John's words, "...*as He is, so are we* in this world" (1 Jn. 4:17b).

Interestingly, the word "servant" appears in the *singular* more than 20 times *before* the grand, pivotal chapter of Isaiah 53 where our Lord is described as the Man of sorrows who was wounded for our transgressions and bruised for our iniquities. (It also predicts His death, burial, and resurrection!)

Is. 53:11, KJV

...by His knowledge shall My righteous servant justify many; for He shall bear their iniquities.

After this great chapter about His cross, Jesus Christ the "servant" (singular) becomes "servants" (the plural, many-membered One)! Jesus, the "corn of wheat" and Pattern Son who fell into the ground and died, has now come forth in glorious resurrection and miraculous multiplication as "the firstborn among *many brethren*" (Jn. 12:24; Rom. 8:29).[12]

Is. 54:17, KJV

*No weapon that is formed against thee shall prosper; and every tongue that shall rise against thee in judgment thou shalt condemn. This is the heritage of the **servants** of the Lord....*[13]

Jesus, the Servant of all, has now become the Lord of all; and His end-time people and brethren are being endued with servant power.

The New Wine Is in the Cluster[14]

Is. 65:8, KJV

> *Thus saith the Lord, As **the new wine is found in the cluster**, and one saith, Destroy it not; for a blessing is in it: so will I do for My servants' sakes, that I may not destroy them all.*

The primary meaning of "cluster" is that of family, togetherness, and the manifold fullness of Christ in His Body.[15] The Hebrew word translated as "cluster" is *'eshkowl*, and it means "a bunch of grapes or other fruit." Its root, *'eshek*, means "to bunch together; a testicle (as a lump)," and is translated as "stone."[16]

Jesus Christ was the "Stone" from Heaven (1 Pet. 2:6) in whom was clustered all the fullness of the Godhead bodily![17] It is He "of whom the whole family in heaven and earth is named" (Eph. 3:15).

The Song of Songs paints an amazing prophetic picture of our beloved Bridegroom as "a *cluster of camphire*" (Song 1:14). The Hebrew word for camphire, *kopher*, is derived from a Hebrew root word meaning "atonement"! Thus our Beloved is "a *cluster of atonement*," revealing His finished work as our Savior. "All the other pieces (experiences) of the Tabernacle furniture could be clustered inside the brazen altar (the cross), prefiguring the scope of the believer's posture *in Christ*...."[18]

The Church, universally and locally, is a cluster of grapes (Is. 65:8)—we are many, yet one (1 Cor. 12:12-27). God sets the solitary in families (Ps. 68:6)—a broken cluster or testicle disqualified one from the priestly ministry (Lev. 21:20). Like the boards of Moses' Tabernacle and the stones of Solomon's Temple, we are framed together as the many-membered Body of Christ. The grapes of Eshcol typify the fruit of the Spirit (Num. 13:23-24; Gal. 5:22-23). The new wine is the joy of the Holy Ghost and the real, reproductive life and strength of God is in the corporate anointing (the bunch of grapes). The family of God is bundled together by the unity of the Spirit in the bond of peace (Eph. 4:1-3). Mature faith and love, the breasts of the Shulamite Bride, are a cluster of grapes (Song 7:7-8; Gal. 5:6; 1 Thess. 5:8). Christ's life is reproduced (as seen in the word "testicle") as we leaven ("lump") the earth as living stones (1 Pet. 2:5).[19]

When you squeeze a real Christian, God comes out! Each of us is a powerful grape, but the abundant fullness of the new wine is still found in the *cluster*.

As the end-time Church moves forward into the next century, we will face many obstacles. In the next ten years, you and I are going to confront some unprecedented challenges.

The anointing upon each of us is powerful. But our greatest hope and confidence is to be a vital part of a *holy cluster*, a divine "they." We will overcome because of our corporate faith, not because of anyone's individual faith.

Other Examples

We have barely sampled the biblical truth concerning corporate expression and anointing. The Bible is filled with example after example of those who flowed together to the goodness of the Lord[20] or suffered together because of corporate complicity in sin:

• The people with one language and speech who gathered together to build the Tower of Babel...

• The curtains of the Mosaic Tabernacle coupled together…

• The army of Joshua marching together in the same direction around Jericho with their mouths shut until it was time to shout…

• The sin of Achan negatively affecting the whole camp, stopping the people in their tracks until sin was dealt with…

• The personal weakness of King Saul overridden by the corporate anointing upon the company of prophets when he prophesied all night…

• David and his men rejoicing and moving together in triumphant procession to bring the Ark of the Covenant to Mount Zion…

• The trumpeters and singers making one sound together in praising and thanking the Lord at the dedication of Solomon's Temple…

• Those singing together at the rededication of the Temple in the Book of Ezra…

• Those families each rebuilding their part of the wall, but then coming together at the sound of the trumpet in the Book of Nehemiah…

• The Jews fasting and praying together as Esther went in unto the King of Persia to deliver her people…

• The 12 apostles of the Lamb together being commissioned by Jesus to preach, teach, and heal…

• The 120 men and women gathering together in the Upper Room awaiting the outpouring of the Holy Ghost…

• The believers in the early Jerusalem Church living together, having all things common…

• The apostles and elders convening together to pool their collective wisdom at the Council of Jerusalem...

• All those who have been raised up and made to sit together in heavenly places in Christ Jesus...

But perhaps the most powerful pattern of corporate anointing in the Bible is found in Exodus 30:22-33—the Mosaic model. It is there that we begin to fully understand the ointment that was compounded "after the art of the apothecary" and used to anoint the whole house of God!

Chapter Four

Corporate Anointing and the Elements of the Apothecary

"And thou shalt make it an oil of holy ointment,
an ointment compound after the art of the apothecary...."

Exodus 30:25

We have explored the wonderful personality of the Anointed One and realized that corporate anointing is exhibited in three dimensions. This glorious mystery, hidden from ages and generations, has now been unveiled to the New Testament people of God as *Christ in and among all of us*.[1] We have already examined some examples of this multi-faceted anointing in the Old and New Testaments. Now we must turn our attention to the "grandfather" of all biblical types and shadows, our chief instructor in the progression of holiness: *the Tabernacle of the congregation*, designed in Heaven by Jehovah and built in the wilderness by Moses and his people.[2]

Principal Spices

Ex. 30:22-25, KJV

Moreover the Lord spake unto Moses, saying,

*Take thou also unto thee **principal spices**, of **pure myrrh** five hundred shekels, and of **sweet cinnamon** half so much, even two hundred and fifty shekels, and of **sweet calamus** two hundred and fifty shekels,*

*And of **cassia** five hundred shekels, after the shekel of the sanctuary, and of **oil olive** an hin:*

And thou shalt make it an oil of holy ointment, an ointment compound after the art of the apothecary: it shall be an holy anointing oil.

The Lord gave Moses a very detailed "recipe" for the compound anointing oil, just as He carefully instructed him concerning every other aspect of the Tabernacle "pattern" (Ex. 25:40). The Hebrew word for "principal" in Exodus 30:23 is *ro'sh*, and it means "head."[3] It is also translated as "beginning, captain, chief, first" in the King James Version. Each of the four "principal" ingredients was a "head" spice! These spices run down from the life of our Head, Jesus Christ, to flow on us, in us, and then through us.

Ps. 133:2, KJV

It [unity] *is like the **precious ointment** upon the head....*

Jn. 3:27, KJV

*...A man can receive nothing, except it **be given him** from heaven.*

Jas. 1:17, KJV

*Every good gift and **every perfect gift is from above**, and cometh down....*

Every believer must learn this principle: The anointing always flows from the Head down!

Jesus Christ is the Head of the Church.[4] He is our great High Priest and the only true Vine, the source of all life.[5] All that we are and all that we have flows down from our ascended Lord. *Each member of Christ's Body is a principal spice, a necessary part, a vital ingredient!* Each of us has derived our ministry gift from Jesus, our glorious Head. Apart from Him, the Fountain of grace, we can do nothing.

The four principal spices—500 shekels of pure myrrh, 250 shekels of sweet cinnamon, 250 shekels of sweet calamus, and 500 shekels of cassia—were compounded and then combined with a hin of olive oil. Each of these elements in God's holy compound were carefully chosen and set apart because of their unique quality, fragrance, or aroma.[6]

First we must understand the numerology of this divine prescription. The total measure of the four elements or ingredients was 1,500 shekels. Fifteen is the biblical number denoting sabbath rest, relegating itself to the Most Holy Place, the realm of Jesus' finished work.[7] Paul the apostle tells us that the mature end-time Church is to come to the fullness of His same "measure" (Eph. 4:13). This truth is also exemplified by the 15 Songs of Degrees in the Psalms and by the 15 steps leading up into the inner sanctuary of Ezekiel's Temple.[8]

Is. 11:1, KJV

And there shall come forth a rod [Jesus] *out of the stem* [David] *of Jesse, and a Branch* [the corporate Body of Christ] *shall grow out of his roots.*

With regard to the principal spices, the symmetry of their four weights (500 plus 250, and 250 plus 500) reminds us of the perfect balance of the seven-branched Golden Lampstand filled with oil. The holy anointing oil was compounded from six units of four raw elements of spice (two parts plus one, one part plus two) which were then crushed and bound together with the "seventh unit" and fifth element, the hin of olive oil. This seven-part compound, like the seven-branched Golden Lampstand, pictures the *sevenfold anointing* that was destined to abide upon Messiah and His Church.[9] This complete anointing is destined to flow through the corporate Man whose name is the "Branch."[10]

The four principal spices plus the oil also picture:

1. The fivefold ascension gift ministries (apostle, prophet, evangelist, pastor, and teacher). They also parallel Aaron and his four sons—Nadab, Abihu, Eleazer, and Ithamar.[11] The New Testament priesthood emphasizes this collective team ministry.

2. The four Gospels followed by the Book of Acts, the latter chronicling the works of the Holy Spirit (symbolized by the oil). Each of the four Gospels, like the four principal spices of the compound anointing, sets forth a different aspect of Jesus' anointed life and ministry.

- The *pure myrrh* of the Gospel of Matthew reveals the King who suffered and died at the hands of His people; He came unto His own and His own received Him not.

- The *sweet cinnamon* of the Gospel of Mark shows the sweetness of the Servant of Jehovah, ever willing to minister to others.

- The *sweet calamus* (which means "branch") of the Gospel of Luke tells of the Man Christ Jesus, the extension and express image of the Father.

- The *cassia* (which means "to cleave") of the Gospel of John illustrates Jesus as the high-flying eagle, the

Pattern Son who soared up to the Father in consummate worship.

As we examine these four principal spices, we do well to note the following:

1. All four blended spices are required to produce the genuine anointing.

2. All four spices are to be at work in every Christian.

3. Each of the four spices indicates the differences among us in the Body of Christ.

4. The first three ingredients were also found in the "garden enclosed" (Song 4:12-14), which pictures Christ in us.[12]

Pure Myrrh

Ex. 30:23, KJV

*Take thou also unto thee principal spices, of **pure myrrh** five hundred shekels....*

The first required principal spice, "pure myrrh," represents *bitter* things or the *sufferings* of the cross of Christ. Because of its priority and prominence, we will deal more with myrrh than with the other three spices.

"Myrrh" is most often translated from the Hebrew word *mor*, and it means "myrrh (as distilling in drops and also as bitter)."[13] Its root word, *marar*, means "to trickle; to be (make) bitter." It is also rendered "vexed, angered, grieved, provoked; gall, temper."[14]

Myrrh may have received its name from the flowing, distilling "tears" (small yellowish or white globules of sap), taken from the gum resin of the shrubby dwarf tree. The small tree, which can reach a height of between eight and nine feet, is found in the Arabian desert and neighboring regions of Africa. It resembles the thorn tree of Egypt. The sap or resin of the myrrh tree flows spontaneously, or the tree could be cut to expedite the process. It has short, stiff, spiny branches, white flowers, and trifoliolate leaves. The gum that exudes from its bark is at first oily, but it becomes hard when it is exposed to the air. The plum-like fruit is smooth and somewhat larger than the pea. Its colors vary from pale reddish-yellow to reddish-brown to red (the color of blood). It has a hard wood and a thorny bark that emits a strong odor.

Myrrh was highly prized, since it was used in incense, perfumes, unguents, and among the Greeks for strengthening wine. The taste of myrrh is bitter, and the substance astringent, acting as an antiseptic disinfectant for wounds and as a stimulant. Myrrh makes a good gargle and mouthwash for sores in the mouth or throat, sore teeth and gums, coughs, asthma, and other chest problems. (Those who have a problem with their breathing—their *prayer life*—need this application of the spice of the cross in their problem areas!)

Notice that the word "pure" is linked with the myrrh. It is translated from the Hebrew *derowr*, which means "(to move rapidly); freedom; hence, spontaneity of outflow, and so clear."[15] It is also rendered in the King James Version as "liberty."[16] Because of its tearful distillation, some have explained "myrrh" to mean "free, or free flowing."

The many uses for myrrh reveal much about our Beloved and His bloody atonement:

1. Myrrh was an *embalming spice* and was used in the embalming of Jesus, showing forth a total death to self.[17]

2. Myrrh was a *preservative*, keeping things from corrupting, rotting, and putrefying, revealing the surety of His divine promises as we are delivered from the corruption of this world.[18]

3. Myrrh *has a beautifying quality*, taking away wrinkles from the face and making the skin smooth and shiny, illustrating the cleansing power of the Word.[19]

4. Myrrh *used in healing* reveals that the anointing brought to us through His passion brings healing and health.[20]

5. Myrrh was a *perfume*, showing that we are to manifest the aroma of the knowledge of Him.[21]

6. Myrrh was a *costly gift fit for the King*, estimating the value of His suffering and the price one will pay to follow Him.[22]

7. Myrrh was *mixed with wine* and offered to Jesus on the cross.[23]

2 Cor. 3:17, KJV

Now the Lord is that Spirit: and where the Spirit of the Lord is, there is liberty.

Pure myrrh was free-flowing. Where the Spirit of the Lord (myrrh) is, there is "liberty."[24] This comes from the Greek word *eleutheria* and its root, which means "freedom...unrestrained (to go at pleasure), (as a citizen) not a slave (whether free born or manumitted), or exempt (from obligation or liability)."[25]

The finished work of the Son of God has made us "free indeed" (Jn. 8:36). The New or Heavenly Jerusalem, the Church, is free.[26] *Corporate anointing* flows freely from those who have identified with His cross.

Song 1:13, KJV

A bundle of myrrh is my wellbeloved unto me; he shall lie all night betwixt my breasts.

This verse deals with the Shulamite's first glimpses concerning the fellowshipping of His sufferings. The word "bundle" points to Jesus' crucifixion—He was helpless, confined, bound. But out of this bundle of death came the "bundle of life" (1 Sam. 25:29)! The Shulamite demonstrates her bridal spirit by her willingness to follow Him at all costs. She has embraced His cross by faith and love—representing total death to self.[27] For you and I, this means His sufferings must penetrate us inwardly until His cross is "wellbeloved."

Many declare the glory of sonship without preaching (by their life and lip) the price of our being heirs of God. They avoid the myrrh of suffering. The phrase "unto me" in Song of Solomon 1:13, "A bundle of myrrh is my wellbeloved *unto* me; he shall lie all night betwixt my breasts," could be rendered "*into* me." The word "lie" reveals His sabbath rest and finished work. Jesus was placed on Calvary *before* He was planted in the heavens.[28] Note the other seven uses of "myrrh" in the Song of Solomon (denoting complete fellowship):

1. The *perfume of suffering* applied in the wilderness (Song 3:6).

2. The *height of suffering* scaled by the pursuit of love (Song 4:6).

3. The *fruit of suffering* grown from within (Song 4:14).

4. The *bread of suffering* gathered by Him and His friends (Song 5:1).

5. The *flow of suffering* dripping from His hand (Song 5:5).

6. The *fragrance of suffering* staining her fingers (Song 5:5).

7. The *purity of suffering* produced by the King's word (Song 5:13).

All of us have experienced some bitter things, and the High Priest of our salvation will mix that into our lives. All great men and women have been processed with myrrh. (I am not speaking about the consequences of lawlessness, of sowing to the wind and then reaping the whirlwind.) Why have some tasted more myrrh than others? Ask the priest. It's tough to pastor during those times because you have no answers. And the last thing anyone needs is to hear some novice spouting off about a lack of faith. *Those who are destined for the heights of Zion will be taken to the depths and plowed.*

The cross is not an option. Everyone will have his *myrrh seasons,* the times of breaking and crushing. Down South, we call it "feeling like you've been pulled through a knot-hole backwards." Before your life and ministry can produce a perfume of pleasure before God, you will ooze and bleed with the fragrance of myrrh. The fellowship of His sufferings is a vital ingredient of the compound anointing.

Sweet Cinnamon

Ex. 30:23, KJV

> *...and of **sweet cinnamon** half so much, even two hundred and fifty shekels....*

The second required principal spice is "sweet cinnamon." It represents *sweet* things, the sweetness of grace.[29] "Cinnamon" is translated from the Hebrew word *qinnamown,* which means "to erect; cinnamon bark (as in upright rolls)."[30] The Greek word for cinnamon, *kinamomon*, appears only in Revelation 18:13.[31] The Hebrew word for "sweet" is *besem* and means "fragrance; spicery."[32]

Cinnamon is a small evergreen tree (symbolizing constant life) that grows to be more than 30 feet tall with stiff leaves, white flowers, and wide-spreading branches. Cinnamon is yellowish-brown with a peculiar, fragrant odor and an aromatic, pungent taste, improving the flavor of bitter substances. Native to Ceylon, the bark and oil of the cinnamon tree was used for the anointing oil and as perfume.

The essence of cinnamon as the sweetness of grace was fulfilled in the life, ministry, and finished work of Christ Jesus. The law came through Moses, but sweet grace and truth were mediated by Jesus Christ, who was sealed and anointed by the Father.[33] Like the sweet psalmist of Israel, Jesus was the anointed of God, Messiah the Prince.[34] The Shulamite bride in the Song of Songs prophetically described Jesus Christ, the One who is altogether lovely, the Husband of the Church: "His cheeks are as a bed of spices, as sweet flowers: His lips like lilies, dropping sweet smelling myrrh. … His mouth is most sweet…" (Song 5:13,16).[35] Jesus' love for us, the gift of Himself for us as a sacrificial offering to the Father, is like a sweet-smelling savor.[36]

As believers, we sit down under the apple tree (Jesus, the Word of God), and His fruit is sweet to our taste.[37] We have become recipients of His anointing, receiving His ability to stay sweet in the bitterest of circumstances.[38]

Cinnamon was one of the nine spices that were found in the garden of the Shulamite.[39] In contrast, man-made religion has perfumed the whorish bed of Babylon with natural sweetness, a cheap imitation.[40] The psalmist, however, declared, "My meditation of Him shall be sweet: I will be glad in the Lord" (Ps. 104:34); and "How sweet are Thy words unto my taste! yea, sweeter than honey to my mouth" (Ps. 119:103)!

God sends happy days just when you need them. The High Priest never neglects to put some sweet cinnamon in your pot. The more pressure you have to deal with, the more cinnamon you need. The sweetness of grace is a must in the life of every believer. God uses the sweet cinnamon of grace to balance the myrrh of suffering, as seen in the consecrated preparation of Queen Esther.[41]

Sweet Calamus

Ex. 30:23, KJV

*...and of **sweet calamus** two hundred and fifty shekels.*

The third required principal spice, "sweet calamus," represents *government* and *divine order*, the extended rule of divine anointing. "Calamus" is translated from the Hebrew word *qaneh*, which means "a reed (as erect); by resemblance a rod (especially for measuring), shaft, tube, stem, the radius (of the arm), beam (of a steelyard)."[42] It is translated in the King James Version as "balance, bone, branch, calamus, cane, reed, stalk." Its root, *qanah*, means "to erect, create; by extension, to procure, especially by purchase (causatively, sell); by implication, to own."[43]

The rod or reed (used for government and measuring) pictured the king's scepter. Calamus is a fragrant, reed-like grass that grows along streams and riverbanks (because it is able to grow in mire), known by some as sweet cane. It scents the air while growing, and was used in the richest perfumes. Calamus leaves are fragrant and ginger-flavored when crushed.

Sweet calamus is prominently pictured in Jesus Christ and in the Word of God. Jesus Christ is the Anointed One, the Messiah. Though bruised in His death, the King stood upright in His resurrection.[44] His life is the extension of the Father's rule and reign. The scepter of His Kingdom is righteousness.[45] This Man is the divine Measure, the anointed Rod or Reed.[46] Jesus "purchased or procured" the Church with His own blood, having given Himself for us as an offering to God for a sweetsmelling savor.[47] Jesus is the central shaft of the Golden Lampstand, uniquely ornamented, the preeminent One.[48]

Jesus is the Vine and we are His branches, the extension of His anointed nature, ministry, and rule. This is prefigured by the six symmetrical branches of the Golden Lampstand.[49] Each of the three branches (on each side) had three sets of ornaments, revealing His nine anointed fruit (nature) and nine gifts of ministry.[50]

Calamus is also one of the nine fruits found in the life of the Shulamite, the type and shadow of the Bride of Christ, the garden of the Lord.[51] Through the promises of the Word, believers have been made partakers of the divine kingly nature.[52]

Calamus scents the air while growing, then is cut down, dried, and powdered to make its rich perfume. Christians bear the sweet savor of Christ even in the crushing times.[53]

The Church constitutes His branches.[54] We are the extension of the Vine, and the government flows from His shoulders and then down to the hand.[55] God is a God of principle. His "due order" (1 Chron. 15:13) sets the leadership and government in the local church, then places the members in their proper place.[56]

With regard to the *charismata*, the grace gifts of the Holy Spirit, everything is to be done decently and in "order" (1 Cor. 14:40). As with the myrrh, the corporate anointing (He, not "it") is free-flowing because the Holy Ghost is a spontaneous river;[57] but He is always between banks. There are measured scriptural principles and parameters that govern the purpose and direction of His life-giving river.[58] In other words, there can be no anointing without discipline.

Prior to her marriage to the king, Queen Esther was anointed and purified for a total of 12 months (six months of myrrh and six months of sweet odors), the biblical number of government and divine order.[59] She listened to the counsel of Hegai (a type of the Holy Spirit), was willing to give her life, and saved her nation. The fragrance of calamus is found in the lives of all those who go before the King. *Lawless people are not anointed.*

Cassia

Ex. 30:24, KJV

*And of **cassia** five hundred shekels....*

The fourth and final required principal spice was "cassia," which represents the true humility of anointed *worship*.

"Cassia" is translated from the Hebrew *qiddah*, which means "cassia bark (as in shrivelled rolls)."[60] Its root, *qadad*, means "to shrivel up, contract or bend the body (or neck) in deference," and is translated in the King James Version as "bow (down) (the) head, stoop."[61] "Cassia" has also been translated "to cleave."

Cassia is a fragrant tree resembling the cinnamon tree, though its bark is less delicate in taste and perfume. This plant has purple flowers and grows at a very high altitude. In addition to its use in the holy anointing oil, cassia was used to scent garments with its perfume.

Jesus Christ, Heaven's Bridegroom, came "out of the ivory palaces" smelling of cassia (Ps. 45:8). He humbled Himself and became obedient to the death of the cross,[62] and the anointing oil was poured on Him as the heavenly Aaron, the Head of the Church.[63] Jesus, as High Priest among His brethren, was sanctified with the oil of gladness above His fellows and was then crowned with His kingly anointing.[64]

Purple speaks of royalty. Christ's regal character is manifested *in us* as kings and priests unto God.[65] Genuine humility enabled by the divine anointing brings promotion in God.[66] The same anointing that scented the garments (ministry) of the Bridegroom will descend upon His Body.[67] We are to have the mind of Christ, the mind of humility.[68]

Those who worship in every circumstance *cling* to God and will not let Him go. We refuse to leave our mate or our local church. Like Jacob in Genesis 32:24-32, princes having His authority will prevail. To persevere and *cleave* is to receive the blessing of His anointing.

The essence of true worship is sacrifice,[69] and true worship is not music. It is the cry of the Son for the Father from the heart.[70] There are three kinds of "worship" in the New Testament that are not acceptable to God:

1. Vain worship (Mt. 15:7-9).

2. Ignorant worship (Acts 17:22-28).

3. Will worship (Col. 2:18-23).

The perfect Worshiper told us that "God is a Spirit: and they that worship Him must worship Him in spirit [from the heart] and in truth [according to the Word of God]" (Jn. 4:24).

The cassia of **true worship** *unlocks and releases all corporate anointing.* Every anointed vessel in the Body of Christ must be a worshiper.

The One Measure and the Beaten Oil That Holds All Together

Ex. 30:24, KJV

...after the shekel of the sanctuary....

All four principal spices were based upon one measure—
"the shekel of the sanctuary." This is a picture of the one true
Measure, the one Canon, the only living Way to the Father—
and His name is Jesus.[71] He is the measure of all "principal"
or "head" spices. All *real anointing* flows out of Him!

This thought is accentuated in the building of the
Tabernacle proper. All its materials were given willingly
with one exception. One-half shekel of silver (the biblical
symbol for redemption) was required of all those 20 years
and older—it was called ransom or atonement money.[72] The
one price of our Redeemer's shed blood is the required standard for all men.[73]

Ex. 30:24, KJV

...and of oil olive an hin.

The myrrh, sweet cinnamon, sweet calamus, and cassia
were compounded and then mingled with olive oil. It was
the oil (a symbol for the Holy Spirit) that activated and
released the ingredients to mix and flow together.[74] Each
and every principal spice was baptized with oil.

The oil was produced by beating the olive berries.[75]
Remember what took place in the Garden of Gethsemane
just before Jesus gave Himself to His accusers, and realize
that Gethsemane means "oil press."[76] It was in the Garden
that Jesus took the cup of bitterness and total self-sacrifice.
It was on the cross that He drank it to the dregs until all was
finished.[77]

These different ingredients of the anointing oil should
remind us of our various ministries.[78] Not everybody is just
like you, nor has everyone been through what you have
experienced. If you understand this, then you won't be so
quick to judge others.

Insecurity is the breeding ground for negative criticism. God anticipates what you need in your life and local church. The art of the apothecary is His alone, and He knows what He's doing. When you have unanswered questions, trust the Great High Priest who foresees what is needed to bring you into your corporate destiny. What upsets most of us is that *we* want to be the chief priest and boss. Stop fretting and wringing your hands. Worry is sin. (The people in the "house" who bother you the most are probably the ones you need the most. Don't be surprised if you discover they are vital ingredients that the Apothecary of Anointing mixed into your life for your perfection!)

Myrrh, cinnamon, calamus, cassia.... Bitter things, sweet things, government, and worship. All four elements must be present in your life and ministry if you are to be truly anointed of God. Some of us may feel that we have had more than our share of one or more of these ingredients. The truth isn't that one of us is *right* and the other *wrong*— we simply are *different* and each is vital to the whole. Our High Priest Jesus, the One who is mixing this heavenly concoction, is the divine Perfumer, the skillful Pharmacist, the appointed and anointed Apothecary.

Chapter Five

Corporate Anointing and the Art of the Apothecary

*"And thou shalt make it an oil of holy ointment,
an ointment compound* after the art of the apothecary:
it shall be an holy anointing oil."

Exodus 30:25

The four principal elements of the Old Testament anointing oil—pure myrrh, sweet cinnamon, sweet calamus, and cassia—were compounded together after the art of the apothecary.

Even as there are different dimensions in our walk with God, so the new birth is only the beginning of our salvation experience. The Pentecostal experience is but the firstfruits of the Spirit and the earnest (pledge) of our inheritance.[1] The fullness of our calling and destiny is a "compound" that is made or created by One greater than us. Even Jesus allowed the Father to mold and shape (to make and compound) His earthly walk.

Every one of us experiences deep dealings as our Father re-creates us in the image of the Pattern Son. Like Enoch of old, we must *learn* to walk with God, and this doesn't happen overnight.[2] It takes many years for the Priest to work these principal spices into our lives and ministries.

Anointing does not automatically fall on us. Somebody has to pay the price to "make it." It will cost you something to love Him and His people.

The Lord commanded Moses, "And thou shalt make it an oil of holy ointment, an ointment compound *after the art of the apothecary*..." (Ex. 30:25). The New International Version calls this "...the work of a perfumer." Only the Lord Jesus can skillfully build the House, His Church.[3] Here is our root principle: The anointing oil was a "compound." This word comes from the Hebrew term *mirqachath*, and it means "an aromatic unguent; also an unguent-pot."[4] Its root word, *raqach*, means "a perfume."[5] It is also translated in the King James Version as "*apothecary*, make (ointment), prepare, spices."

Many may be tempted to overlook the little word "art" in Exodus 30:25. They shouldn't. It is translated from the Hebrew word *ma'aseh*, and it means "operative; action, activity."[6] It is also translated as "act, business, deed, doing, labor, thing made, occupation, workmanship, wrought" in the King James Version.[7] This "art of the apothecary" involves divine operations, actions, and activity!

We Do Not "Stir" the Pot—We Are "in" the Pot

When the apostle Paul wrote to the Corinthians regarding the *corporate ministry* in the Body of Christ, he declared that there were different giftings, ministries, and anointings, and added, "But it is the same God which *worketh* all in all" (1 Cor. 12:6b). This is the Greek word *energeo*, which means "to be active, efficient; to be effectual (fervent), be mighty in, shew forth self, work (effectually in)."[8]

I beseech every preacher to hear me. You and I are not "stirring" this holy pot—we are *in* the pot! Jesus the Priest is creating a Holy Ghost chemistry among all of us.

The office and function of the "apothecary" appears ten times in the Old Testament.[9] It was the art of the apothecary to "compound" the holy anointing oil for the anointing of priests, utensils, and furniture; and to "temper together" the incense that was offered exclusively to Jehovah before the Testimony of the Most Holy Place.[10] In both cases, the art of the apothecary was to "rub to pieces or pulverize" the elements of the anointing oil and the incense or perfume. Both were a masterful blend, a divine concoction.[11]

When these ingredients were properly crushed or "beaten small" and joined, they *together* produced a medicine. It was understood that the priestly apothecary, the perfumer, was a medicine man.

Certain ingredients in you will release the divine substance in others. This kind of interaction and "cross-pollination" cannot happen in any other kind of environment. For example, each of us is called to be a worshiper;[12] yet something happens in *corporate* praise and worship that cannot take place in any other way.

We have to get this mixture just right. Think about the familiar advertising phrase from the commercial product called "Alka-seltzer": "...Plop, plop; fizz, fizz..." You don't activate this antacid by keeping it in the medicine cabinet or by putting it in your mouth. You have to drop it into water and allow it to dissolve to release the remedy contained in the medicine.

Each of us needs to open up to sweeten this pot. Let God crush your spice so that you can be mingled with others. Let Him flow through you. Your personal anointing is destined to be joined with the corporate—you are a unique substance of fabulous worth!

God's emphasis—the Divine Apothecary's emphasis—is not that you are a *particular* member, but that you are a *member* (a co-mingled ingredient) in particular. Your chief joy isn't that you have unique gifts or qualities, but that you have been selected and included in God's pot for the concoction of His divine anointing oil. You cannot make any of the four principal spices, but you can willingly rendezvous your portion with your brother's.

This apothecary theme runs throughout the Bible. A compound is always a greater substance in power and quality than one ingredient by itself—just as it takes water, sand, and gravel in union with crushed portland cement to make solid concrete.

Mankind himself is like reconstituted lemon juice. By ourselves, we are sour. God adds water and sugar to make refreshing lemonade. We are depleted. We are hewed-down man—we are human. We need to be made replete by His Word and Spirit.

The "Year of Jubilee" was actually a *compound* of sabbaths, when both the land and the people would take a sabbath rest from certain labor, debt, or bondages.[13] Jesus Christ is our living Jubilee.

God Himself is "one Lord" (Deut. 6:4),[14] and He is not fragmented. Though He is one, and though He Himself is an Apothecary, He reveals Himself in the New Testament as Father, Son, and Holy Spirit;[15] and as Spirit, light, love, and a consuming fire.[16]

Consider God's goodness and chastisement, His severity and mercy, His death, burial, and resurrection—these are compounds. Have you ever thought about the "wrath of the Lamb" (Rev. 6:16)? How could Jesus have turned water into wine in John 2? The answer is found in one of the Greek words for "agree," *sumphoneo*. This is the root of our English word "symphony," and means "to be harmonious, to sound together."[17] Why is it that men only want to "make symphony" or agree when they are desperate?

The psalmist declared, "Mercy and truth are *met together*; righteousness and peace have *kissed* each other" (Ps. 85:10). These all exemplify the art of the apothecary (although the Bible also tells us that some things do not mix in Deuteronomy 22:9-11 and Galatians 5:17).

The Greatest Example of the Apothecary's Art

The greatest example of the apothecary art is the mystery of His incarnation.[18] Jesus is both "white and ruddy" (Song 5:10), representing the miraculous mingling of divinity and humanity—Jesus was very God and very man! When the Word was made flesh, He interfaced two worlds, the invisible and the visible. He is the living Door joining Heaven and earth. Our King is the color purple, the blending of blue (heavenly) and red (earthly). The first Adam turned the Garden into a graveyard. The last Adam turned the graveyard into a garden!

The Whole House Is Anointed

Ex. 30:26-28, KJV

> And **thou shalt anoint the tabernacle** of the congregation therewith, and **the ark of the testimony**,
>
> And **the table** and **all his vessels**, and **the candlestick** and **his vessels**, and **the altar of incense**,

> And **the altar of burnt offering** with **all his vessels**, and **the laver** and his foot.

These verses underscore one great truth: The *whole house* (tabernacle) and *everything in it* was to be anointed with the holy anointing oil!

First, from a Christ-centered viewpoint, we must understand that to anoint each piece of furniture in the Tabernacle *is to anoint the Lord Himself*! To pour oil on the Ark of the Covenant is to exalt the Lord and King in all His glory. To anoint the table of shewbread is to glorify Him who is the Word of God. To consecrate the candlestick is to magnify Him who is the source of all light and revelation. To anoint the altar of incense is to pour out oil on our prayer, praise, and worship to Him and of Him. To pour oil on the brazen altar is to prioritize His finished work on the cross. To anoint the laver is to release Him who is made unto us sanctification.

When we anoint the Head first,[19] He mixes and changes the very atmosphere. As we focus on Jesus, the ointment compounded becomes concentrated, becoming ever stronger and more potent to remove burdens and destroy yokes.

A great house holds many kinds of vessels,[20] just as every local church holds many different kinds of people having different gifts, who are also at different levels or places in their walk with God. My prayer is that each of us will say, "The whole house is anointed, and because I am part of the house, I am anointed!" When you pour oil on others, you pour oil on yourself.

The Scripture passage in Exodus 30:26 quoted earlier mentions the "ark of the testimony" found in the Most Holy Place, and verse 27 mentions the furniture of the Holy Place—the table, the candlestick, and the altar of incense. The following verse mentions the altar of burnt offering and the laver of the Outer Court. All three courts were to be anointed.

In the second chapter of this book, we explained that the "excellent things" were to be "threefold things" according to Proverbs 22:20. There we discovered afresh that God's purposes are revealed in three levels.

According to Exodus 30, all three portions of the Tabernacle or house of God—the Outer Court, Holy Place, and Most Holy Place, along with the pieces of furniture and instruments in each—were anointed with the *same* oil!

Evangelicals, Pentecostals, and those who want the high calling into Zion are all daubed with the same Spirit![21] There is no "big" Holy Ghost for one group and a little" Holy Ghost for a "lesser" group! Little children, young men, and fathers are all anointed.[22]

His "name is as ointment poured forth" (Song 1:3)—the same name of Jesus has been invoked over us all! The same Lord over all is rich unto all.[23] The same anointing…the same Spirit…the same name…

It's a different *measure*,[24] but it's the *same oil*—the whole house and everything in it is anointed! The whole house—the whole city, county, state, nation, eventually the whole earth—will be anointed![25]

Ex. 30:29-30, KJV

> *And thou shalt sanctify **them**, that **they** may be most holy: **whatsoever toucheth them shall be holy**.*
>
> *And thou shalt **anoint Aaron and his sons**, and consecrate them, that they may minister unto Me in the priest's office.*

Notice that God used the words "them" and "they." This underscores the fact that God was commissioning a *corporate operation.* Everything that touched "*them*" shall be "holy" (Ex. 30:29).[26] Remember that this passage is but a type and shadow of the greater reality taking place in your life right now as a member of His Body in particular! This corporate anointing will rub off on everyone and everything *you* touch too! Go ahead. Be a blessing in your family, your local church, and your community. Lose your pride. Identify with something bigger than yourself. Touch somebody, and let somebody touch you. *Together*, we are more contagious than any infectious disease!

The command to anoint "Aaron and his sons" involved five people: Aaron the high priest plus Eleazer, Ithamar, Nadab, and Abihu. These men were consecrated or cleansed for the priest's office. These Levites prefigure the "royal priesthood" of the New Testament (1 Pet. 2:9).[27] The five of them, together consecrated for ministry to God and His people, point prophetically to the apostle, prophet, evangelist, pastor, and teacher—the fivefold ministries—the dream team that flows from the ascended Christ.[28] The words "unto Me" in Exodus 30:30 reiterate that the corporate anointing is to be poured out upon the Head first.

Neither Shall Ye Make Any Other Like It

Ex. 30:31-32, KJV

And thou shalt speak unto the children of Israel, saying, This shall be an holy anointing oil unto Me throughout your generations.

Upon man's flesh shall it not be poured....

It is significant that this holy compound oil was prescribed "throughout" Israel's generations. Why? Because it is yet another confirmation that the anointing (the Anointed One) transcends time and space and spans the ages (we will look closer at this in a later chapter).

It is also important to realize that there are vital *limitations* placed upon the corporate anointing that we need to observe. Anyone who violated God's guidelines concerning this anointing oil was literally cut off from the Old Testament congregation physically and spiritually.

First, God's special corporate anointing was never to be poured on the flesh of "man" or "adam." The New Testament reality of this Old Testament command is seen in Romans 8:6 where Paul wrote, "For to be carnally [selfishly, individually] minded is death; but to be spiritually minded [or corporately minded, as a member of Christ's Body] is life and peace." Another picture of this is seen in the days of Noah, which prefigured the endtimes.[29] When Noah released the dove (a symbol of the Holy Spirit) from the ark to seek out land, it would not light upon *dead flesh* floating atop the waters of judgment. How many times have we tried to persuade God's Spirit to alight on our dead works (and meetings) of the flesh? It just won't happen. God will only anoint Himself.

Ex 30:32-33, KJV

> *...neither shall ye make any other like it, after the composition of it: it is holy, and it shall be holy unto you.*
>
> *Whosoever compoundeth any like it....*

Second, the "composition" of the corporate anointing *was not to be imitated*. The original Hebrew word translated as "composition" means "proportion (in size, number, or ingredients)," and comes from a root meaning "to balance, measure out."[30] In other words, this secret compound had a divine patent. "It is holy, and *it shall be holy unto you*." With this blunt statement, God was making it clear that He expected His people to share His attitude toward the holy and exclusive nature of the anointing He was giving to them. Nothing has changed in our day. The anointing is *still holy*.

Prov. 7:16, KJV

I have decked my bed with coverings of tapestry, with carved works, with fine linen of Egypt.

There are two women in the Book of Proverbs, the strange woman and the virtuous woman.[31] There are also two women pictured in the Book of Revelation, the harlot and the Bride.[32] Whether the eternal types and shadows are applied to an unsaved girlfriend or to an adulterous religious system that has reveled in the works and lusts of the flesh, the "strange" or "foreign, profane, adulterous" woman of Proverbs 7 represents anyone or anything that tries to flatter and seduce the child of God.

This proverbial harlot is especially skilled at enticing young people (or believers) who are "simple" or "silly, foolish, open, deluded"—or the immature described in Proverbs 7:7 as those who are "void of understanding." This harlot decks or spreads her bed (because she wants to "reproduce" her damnation) with "coverings of tapestry" and the "fine linen of Egypt" (Prov. 7:16). This may allude to the Egyptian practice of wrapping mummies; in spiritual terms, it speaks of *man-made righteousness*.

Money-grabbers in the trappings of the fivefold office will imitate the anointing to keep the saints in a constant state of need. In stark contrast, a real and true ministry descended from the Head will give men the Word of God and then wean them unto making their own wise choices. Everything that men have brought forth in His name *that God did not tell them to produce* is being shaken out of His Kingdom.[33] The consequences for profaning God's holy anointing have always been severe, but God has "raised the ante." The spiritual consequences far outweigh the physical consequences prescribed under the Law of Moses: The harlot and her bed shall be burned with fire.[34]

Prov. 7:17, KJV

*I have **perfumed** my bed with **myrrh**, aloes, and **cinnamon**.*

When men do not understand the *corporate* Christ, they might as well say (along with the harlot) that the "goodman is not at home" (Prov. 7:19).[35] The harlot has perfumed her bed with an illegal imitation, using but two of the four primary ingredients required for the compound anointing. (Once you have perceived the corporate nature of Christ's Body, you will never be satisfied with an incomplete, cheap imitation.) This kind of adulterous seduction is always motivated by an unholy spirit, because the harlot's love potion and illegal concoction was made without the beaten olive oil (a symbol for the Holy Spirit). Throughout the Bible era, the apothecary (a trained professional, and usually a priest) also made *embalming fluid*! Some believe that this verse in Proverbs alludes to its concoction for the seduction and destruction of the unwise.[36]

Is your apothecary creating sweet oil or embalming fluid? Is your ministry better or bitter? Are you ministering life or death to others? Anyone who is not working for corporate unity and compound anointing is creating a *cheap imitation*. They are agreeing with disunity, in direct disobedience to the commands of Jesus and the desire of the Father. They are scattering the saints, not gathering them.[37] These ministries of death are killing people with a half-hearted obedience toward divine order and pattern.

Making a Witches' Brew

The Greek word for "sorceries" used in the New Testament is *pharmakeia*, and it means "a drug, spell-giving potion." Its root word means "a druggist ('pharmacist') or poisoner; a magician."[38] It is listed in the King James Version as "witchcraft" among the works of the flesh;[39] and as you already know, witchcraft is rebellion.[40]

Ex. 30:33, KJV

...or whosoever putteth any of it upon a stranger, shall even be cut off from his people.

Third, the corporate anointing was not to be put on a "stranger." The original Hebrew term seems to define a "stranger" as "a foreigner, strange, profane; specifically (active participle) to commit adultery."[41] This describes people or ideas that are estranged from the holy covenant, who are separated from true praise and worship, the local church, tithing, Christ-like service to others, and so forth.

Don't put the holy oil of the Anointed One on a stranger. Don't lay hands on a man "suddenly" or "speedily, hastily." Instead, make sure you know those who labor among you.[42]

Dead Flies in the Ointment

Eccles. 10:1, KJV

Dead flies cause the ointment of the apothecary to send forth a stinking savour: *so doth a little folly him that is in reputation for wisdom and honour.*

An apothecary can mix anointing oil or witches' brew. And even a faithful apothecary who fails to "cover" his prepared ointment in prayer can have the ointment of the corporate anointing *profaned* and spoiled by "dead flies," the devices of beelzebub ("lord of flies" or the "dung-god").[43] As these bad words, deeds, and spirits gush forth, they emit a foul odor, the savor of death. The Hebrew term translated as "stinking savour" means "to smell bad; figuratively, to be offensive morally."[44] It could be interpreted as "sending forth an abominable spirit."

A man or woman who leads others is held in "reputation" or is "valuable." The devil knows that just a little (or a few acts of) "folly" or "silliness" will *spoil* their spices. Preacher, be careful! Just a little marginal silliness will give a bad smell. In those weak areas of our lives, the "fool" in us wants to say, "There is no God" (Ps. 14:1).

There are other flies waiting to spoil and contaminate the corporate anointing too. Solomon warned us about "servants upon horses, and princes walking as servants" in Ecclesiastes 10:7. This speaks of homes, local churches, cities, or nations that are devoid of divine order and government.

When the laity or some board rules the man or woman of God, the Head is out of place—so the flow of the anointing ceases.[45] Flipping that over, when leadership follows the way of error and the doctrine of Balaam by preaching for reward and loving the wages of unrighteousness, then their ministry stinks of the influence of the "dung-god."[46] All these things are wrong ingredients. There's nothing but death in that pot.[47]

Dead flies are removed from the precious ointment of the apothecary by means of prayer, praise, and worship. One of the ingredients for the incense that was used on the Golden Altar of incense was the odorous gum galbanum.[48] Perhaps it is no accident that this powerful aromatic was used to drive away insects or reptiles! At the same time, the sweet aroma of true prayer and praise and worship will permeate the atmosphere with the sweetness of corporate anointing and drive away every foul odor and influence from the fallen prince of the power of the air.

We have examined the ingredients, the application, and the prohibitions concerning the Levitical apothecary. The

Mosaic model has served as the foundation for our study of the compound or corporate anointing. Now we will follow Moses and His people as they journey toward the Promised Land. When Doctor Luke wrote the Book of Acts, he called this Old Testament nation "the church in the wilderness" (Acts 7:38).

Chapter Six

Corporate Anointing and the Church in the Wilderness

"…all our fathers…."

1 Corinthians 10:1

The wisest ones among us understand the value of learning from the past. This is especially true in the Kingdom of God. The Pentateuch, the first five books of the Bible and the Jewish Scriptures, tell the story of what Stephen described as "the church in the wilderness" in his final address before the Jewish Sanhedrin in Acts 7:38.[1]

The "church in the wilderness" is a prophetic picture of the Body called out of bondage and into promise. Although it literally refers to Moses and Israel in the wilderness, it also speaks to the Body "called out" today, the Church of the Risen King.

1 Cor. 10:1-4, KJV

*Moreover, brethren, I would not that ye should be ignorant, how that **all** our fathers were under the cloud, and **all** passed through the sea;*

*And were **all** baptized unto Moses in the cloud and in the sea;*

*And did **all** eat the same spiritual meat;*

*And did **all** drink the same spiritual drink: for they drank of that spiritual Rock that followed them: and that Rock was Christ.*

1 Cor. 10:11, KJV

*Now all these things happened unto them for **ensamples: and they are written for our admonition, upon whom the ends of the world are come**.*

Everything that has happened and all that has been written have been provided as examples and warnings for the end-time people of God! The literal Greek reading of "these things *happened*" says, "these things *walked together*...."[2] History is a living thing. History itself is anointed. According to the Word of God, all these Old Testament events worked and "walked together" into our day to speak to us.

These events are "ensamples" or examples for us, but the original Greek word, *tupos*, is much stronger than "example." It means "a die (as struck), a stamp or scar; by analogy, a shape...a model (for imitation) or instance (for warning)."[3]

The Old Testament nation was a type of the New Testament "holy nation" that would follow (1 Pet. 2:9). For this reason, the admonition of the Pentateuch *has much to teach us* by reminding us of the lessons learned (and not learned) by those who went before us.[4] We are the people upon whom the "end" or the goal, the final conclusion, and ultimate purpose of the world or age has come.[5]

We need to learn five crucial lessons from the experiences of the Church in the wilderness under the headship of Moses. We will cover all but one of these in this chapter:

The Church in the wilderness was...

1. *Kept* during the hour of trial (Ex. 7–12).

2. *Delivered* by blood, water, and Spirit (Ex. 12–15).

3. *Supernaturally supplied* (Ex. 16–17).

4. *Instructed* (Ex. 18–40; Lev. 1–27; Num. 1–10; Deut. 4–33).

5. *Sifted* (Num. 11–17).

God Begins His Purpose With a Man

Jn. 1:6, KJV

There was a man sent from God....

God begins His design with a man (or woman), and then consummates His purpose in and through a nation or people. For instance, Jehovah initiated His Old Testament objective to deliver Israel from bondage with Moses, and then multiplied Moses into a nation. He led His man as a *patterned example* into the wilderness for 40 years, and then took the nation into that same place of testing for 40 more years.

The Law came through Moses, but Jesus Christ mediated grace and truth.[6] Moses was the Old Testament middleman, but now there is one New Testament Mediator between God and men, the Man Christ Jesus.[7] Jesus is the Prophet who was raised up like unto Moses and was led into the desert of temptation for 40 days before beginning His great work of eternal deliverance.[8]

The first six chapters of the Book of Exodus describe in detail how God raised up His man through stringent preparation. At one time, God even sought to kill Moses because he failed to circumcise his son according to the Abrahamic covenant![9]

Moses made four objections to his calling that are still echoed by reluctant "called out ones" in our day.

1. A lack of qualifications: "Who am I?" (Ex. 3:11) He felt unable to perform the task ordained of God. God's answer was *and is*: "Certainly I will be with thee" (Ex. 3:12).

2. A lack of subject matter: "What shall I say?" (Ex. 3:13) Moses was afraid he would be unable to reply to the questions that would surely come. God's answer was *and is*: "Say...I AM hath sent me" (Ex. 3:14).

3. A lack of credentials: "They will not believe me" (Ex. 4:1). Moses was convinced he would be unable to convince others of his divine appointment. God's answer was *and is*: "What is that in thine hand?" (Ex. 4:2)

4. A lack of eloquence: "I am not eloquent" (Ex. 4:10). Moses felt disqualified because he was unable to express himself with the eloquence of men. God's answer was *and is*: "I will be with thy mouth, and teach thee what thou shalt say" (Ex. 4:12).

In one of the most astounding prophetic events of the Old Testament, Jehovah later imparted the spirit of Moses onto the 70 elders, and Moses became *a many-membered corporate man*, prefiguring the mystery of the corporate Church.[10] Likewise, the Father has sent forth the Spirit of His Son into our hearts, thus multiplying His firstborn Son into many brethren.[11] As we learned in previous chapters, "Christ" is now *more than an individual* in the earth. He is both Head and Body, one glorious new creation Man.

God has raised up a corporate Man with a corporate anointing. The name of this corporation is "Christ." This many-membered Man with Jesus as the Head has legal ownership of all things.[12] According to God's Word, the earth belongs to "Mr. and Mrs. Jesus Christ"![13]

Consider the Old Testament pattern fulfilled in the New Covenant of Christ: In Exodus 1–6, God got His man. He always does. When the rod of Moses became the rod of God, then by divine design, the God *in* Moses became "god" unto Pharaoh (Ex. 7:1)! Now put the Church, the Body of Christ, in Moses' place in this pattern, and you suddenly begin to see the mystery of the Church revealed in the earth.

Kept During the Hour of Trial

Whether you are dealing with eschatology or daily practicalities, this biblical principle remains constant: God doesn't take His people out of pressures and trials; He *keeps* His people *through* them!

Just as the plagues came upon Egypt, so our nation and the world are being judged. The nations are mad, rushing on in a blind fury.[14] Pharaoh's days are numbered. There are no answers. Mankind is at its wits' end. Every bit of human wisdom and genius has failed to find solutions. Why? Because there can be no peace apart from the Prince of peace. The messenger of death is passing through the nations, and homes are being ripped asunder by the devourer. Our only hope is the blood of the Passover Lamb.

Under the leadership of Moses, the Old Testament nation learned to endure in the time of trouble. We too must come into a living experience of knowing the Lord who is the keeper of His pavilion. We must walk in the secret of His presence and His tabernacle. We must know that He will take care of us.

Many Christians in America have never trusted God to meet their needs. Their faith is soft, pampered, and luke-warm through lack of exercise and exposure to genuine pressure.[15] They want nothing to do with the thought of hardship or tribulation, yet God is raising up a people who "know Him" and will trust Him to keep them during the hour of trial.[16] Society is crumbling. Babylon is falling. This world system, like the boat carrying the apostle Paul in Acts 27, is headed for the rocks. But we need to remember that when God judged Egypt, He preserved His people!

There were ten plagues that fell upon the land of Ham, and these signs and wonders were "tools of emancipation" to deliver God's people from Egypt's enslavement.[17] They manifested or revealed the power or "finger of God" to the defiant captor holding His people in bondage.[18] These plagues were the fruit of God's judgment and divine wrath upon Pharaoh, his kingdom, and the false gods of Egypt.[19] Above all, these scourges demonstrated that Jehovah was high above all gods and constituted a solemn warning to other nations.[20]

The progressive nature of the severity of these plagues provides a vivid description of the world system (typified by Egypt).

- The water turned into blood tells of death covering the world.

- The multiplying of the frogs speaks of unclean spirits in the world.

- The lice reveal the world's uncleanness and filth.

- The swarms of flies describe the sons of beelzebub (satan).

- The murrain reveals that the service of the natural man is corrupted.

- The boils describe the condition of the worldly.[21]

- The hail tells us that the wrath of God abides upon the disobedient.

- The locusts speak of the barren desolation of worldly living.

- The darkness tells us that the world is void of and alienated from the light.

- The death of the firstborn points to the second death.[22]

The first three plagues were unique in two ways. First, the magicians of Egypt *duplicated* some of these early and "lesser" miracles, but they were powerless to go beyond this point![23]

Second, the first three plagues fell on the *children of Israel* as well as upon the Egyptians! After this, God *kept His own* during the hour of trial, enabling them to walk in spiritual immunity. Moses and Aaron (symbolizing the king-priest principle) brought tribulation upon *all men* to deliver a chosen few. Two old men had walked out of the wilderness with just a stick between them, and the younger of them was 80. Jehovah wanted to establish in the hearts of His people that these chosen deliverers, these two witnesses, were sent from God. At this stage, He had to convince those who were *His own people* as well as those who were not.

Israel was protected and kept by the power of God during this time of judgment, and He will do no less for us in this day.[24] God is not going to "take us out" to protect us, because He intends to *bring us through* instead as an even greater demonstration of His supreme power.[25]

Ex. 8:22-23, KJV

*And I will **sever** in that day the land of Goshen, in which My people dwell, that no swarms of flies shall be there; to the end thou mayest know that I am the Lord in the midst of the earth.*

> *And I will put a **division** between My people and thy people: to morrow shall this sign be.*

When Moses delivered this word from the Lord to Pharaoh, the Lord used the word "sever." The original Hebrew word means "to distinguish." It is also rendered in the King James Version as "put a difference, separate, set apart....to be distinct, or marked out, to discriminate."[26] It means that Israel was *separated unto God* in a distinguishing, marvelous manner.

The Hebrew word translated as "division" in Exodus 8:23 means "distinction, deliverance." It is also translated as "redeem, redemption" in the King James Version. It comes from a root word meaning "to project, precede; hence, to anticipate, hasten, meet (usually for help)."[27]

God makes a difference. He *hastens* to meet the needs of His people. He kept the Church in the wilderness during the hour of trial, but *He also separates* the sheep from the goats. Like Boaz, our Kinsman-Redeemer, Jesus Christ, is down at the threshingfloor dividing His harvest.[28] God is both sanctifying (or separating for holy purposes) and protecting His own.

Delivered by Blood, Water, and Spirit

Paul declared that after God kept the Church in the wilderness during the hour of trial in Egypt, "all our fathers" who had been delivered by the blood of the Passover lamb were "baptized" in the "cloud" and in the "sea" (1 Cor. 10:1-2). He went on to say that "all" of them *corporately* ate the *same spiritual food* and drank the *same spiritual drink*. Look at these examples now and we will examine their significance in a moment. *All* shared in...

1. The blood of the Passover Lamb (Ex. 12).

2. The baptism into Moses in the sea (Ex. 14–15).

3. The baptism into Moses in the cloud (Ex. 13).

4. The bread—the manna from Heaven (Ex. 16).

5. The beverage—the water from the flinty rock (Ex. 17).

As we relate these Old Testament examples to our Christian experience, the first three experiences are types and shadows of events that occur "once and for all" in our life in Jesus Christ: our baptism in the blood of the Lamb, our baptism in the water, and our baptism in the Holy Spirit.

The other two corporate experiences reflect ongoing events in our lives as disciples of Christ and members of His Body, the Church. We are to eat "the Bread of life" daily by reading and meditating on the Word of God.[29] In the same way, we must drink daily of the life of the Spirit of Christ springing up from within.[30]

All the Old Testament fathers were delivered by the blood. When God was ready to bring His nation out of bondage, *He put a lamb in every house.* Under the New Covenant, He has again *put the Lamb in every house, or temple of the heart.* Jesus Christ, the spotless Lamb of God, is the complete fulfillment of this type.[31] The blood was not an option—*everyone* who came out of Egypt was delivered by nothing less than the blood. In the same way, it is through the blood of the Lamb that we have been set free from the bondage of this world, of sin, and of satan. We have been brought out of darkness and into His marvelous light.[32]

1 Cor. 10:2, KJV

*And were **all baptized** unto Moses **in the cloud** and **in the sea**.*

In this first significant baptism, "all" the fathers passed through the Red Sea, and were baptized "unto" or "into" Moses.[33] We have also been *baptized in water* in the name of the Lord Jesus Christ for the remission of our sins and the circumcision of our hearts.[34] Pharaoh was a type of the god and prince of this world, and when Israel left Pharaoh's territory, he and his army foolishly tried to pursue them unto the Red Sea. It was there—in the midst of the baptism of separation by water—that the power and might of Egypt's king was broken forever.[35] Paul explained in Romans 6:1-14 that the authority of sin and satan no longer have dominion over those who have been *baptized into Christ,* who fully identify with His death, burial, and resurrection. We have died to sin and have arisen to walk in newness of life!

Next, "all" the members of the Church in the wilderness were baptized into Moses in "the cloud" in Exodus 13. This is a picture of the Pentecostal experience, the Holy Ghost baptism.[36] We are to be filled with the Holy Spirit, as were the early believers in the Book of Acts. By one Spirit are we all baptized into one Body.[37] Again, this experience is not the fullness of the Spirit, but it represents the *firstfruits* of the Spirit and the earnest of our inheritance.[38]

So the Church in the wilderness was delivered by the blood, the water, and the Spirit. The apostle John summarized this understanding when he said, "And there are three that bear witness in earth, the spirit, and the water, and the blood: and these three agree in one" (1 Jn. 5:8).

Supernaturally Supplied

We have been kept during the hour of trial. We are a New Testament people, brought into the New Covenant by the blood, the water, and the Spirit. God has *saved* and *delivered* us, and He will continue to take care of us just as He supernaturally supplied every need of the Church in the wilderness.

Many believers suppose that this "supernatural supply" refers to material things and what money can buy, but Paul had something else in mind.

1 Cor. 10:3, KJV

*And did **all** eat the **same spiritual meat**.*

The Old Testament nation was supernaturally supplied two things vital to life:

1. *By the manna*, the bread from Heaven: *the Word* (Ex. 16).

2. *By the water* from the flinty rock: *the Spirit* (Ex. 17).

To partake of the manna, the same spiritual meat, is to feed on the Word of God every day.[39]

Mt. 4:4, KJV

> *...Man shall not live by bread alone, but by every word that **proceedeth** out of the mouth of God.*

There is a "preceding" word, and there is a "proceeding" word. God *has* spoken unto us, but He *is* speaking to us today as well. The proceeding word today builds upon the sure foundation of the preceding word received by men of God "as they were moved by the Holy Ghost" yesterday (2 Pet. 1:21). God's prophetic words today bring glorious application to the "more sure word of prophecy" received in the canonical Scriptures (2 Pet. 1:19).[40] We are established in "present truth" as the Spirit speaks to the Church today (2 Pet. 1:12).[41]

The word "manna" is literally a question. It means "a whatness; what?; what is it?"[42] It is mentioned 14 times in the Old Testament (the biblical number denoting salvation), and five times in the New Testament (the number for grace). The Bible calls it God's manna; bread *from* Heaven and the bread *of* Heaven; the corn of Heaven; and angels' food.[43] Paul called it "spiritual meat" (1 Cor. 10:3).

God's instructions for gathering the manna were explicit, and every description of the manna points to Jesus Christ, the living Word.[44] He is our suitable, sufficient, satisfying, sustaining, sure, and strengthening portion. Manna was:

1. Small (Ex. 16:14): *humble*.

2. Round (Ex. 16:14): *perfect*.

3. Hoar frost (Ex. 16:14): *fresh*.

4. White (Ex. 16:31): *holy*.

5. Coriander seed (Ex. 16:31): *fragrant*.

6. Honey (Ex. 16:31): *sweet*.

7. Color of bdellium (Num. 11:7): *precious*.

8. Taste of fresh oil (Num. 11:8): *authoritative*.

9. Dew on it and under it (Num. 11:9): *Spirit-filled*.

The sheer volume of the daily provision of manna in the wilderness points to God's bountiful and unfailing supply. God provided a miraculous provision of "an omer" (six pints) of manna per man per day. For three million people, the rate would be 18 million pints (*over 13 million pounds*) per day. This is almost 7,000 tons! If we were to provide a single day's supply of manna for that number of people today, it would take *15 trains, each having 30 cars, and each car holding 15 tons*!

God's Word is enough...

1 Cor. 10:4, KJV

> And did **all drink** the **same spiritual drink**: for they drank of that **spiritual Rock** that followed them: and **that Rock was Christ**.

Jesus Christ is the Rock who was smitten "once and for all" on Calvary's cross. Now all we have to do is *speak* to the Rock and He will minister life.[45] Ever since Jesus finished His work on the cross, God has supernaturally supplied His Church with "spiritual drink" by the Spirit from within. The water flowing from the "flinty rock" is a type of the indwelling Christ, and many Old Testament passages tell about the water from the Rock.[46] Believers need to drink from the midst of the Rock every day by praying in the Holy Ghost.[47]

Jn. 4:14, KJV

> *But whosoever **drinketh of the water that I shall give** him shall never thirst; but **the water that I shall give him** shall be in him a well of water **springing up** into everlasting life.*

Jn. 7:38-39, KJV

> *He that believeth on Me, as the scripture hath said, **out of his belly shall flow rivers of living water.***
>
> (But this spake He of the Spirit...).*

Instructed

The first six chapters of the Book of Exodus are devoted to the story of *how God got His man* (Ex. 1–6). The next six chapters tell us how Jehovah *kept His people* through Egypt's tribulation (Ex. 7–12). Four chapters demonstrate how Israel was *delivered by the blood, the water, and the Spirit* (Ex. 12–15). The next two chapters describe how God *supernaturally supplied* bread from Heaven and water from the rock (Ex. 16–17). What follows all that?

I find it interesting that most of remaining chapters of the Pentateuch carry one primary thought: *they were instructed.*[48]

It took God 17 chapters to get His people *kept, delivered*, and *supplied*. (These are the same things, especially in a material sense, that seem to preoccupy the majority of American Christians.) Now I want you to notice something of critical importance: Israel knew God's acts, but Moses *knew His ways.*[49]

The Holy Ghost inspired Moses to record *90 more chapters* to indoctrinate Israel on how to walk in the paths of the Lord. That is a strong indication that *God is almost five times more interested in teaching us than He is in meeting our needs!* He is apostolic before He is pastoral. He knows it is far more important to build His own *nature and character* into us than to merely keep us, deliver us, or supply us! (If we have His nature and character, then the rest follows naturally, as Jesus said in Matthew 6:33.)

The remainder of the Book of Exodus lays out the Decalogue (the Ten Commandments) and many other laws besides.[50] But mostly it deals with the divine "pattern" of the Tabernacle of Moses and the garments of the high priest.[51] Added to the whole Tabernacle scheme is the Levitical priesthood, the five major offerings, and the seven Feasts of Jehovah recorded in the Books of Leviticus and Deuteronomy. All these grand and glorious themes were for the *instruction* of Israel.

To sum up all this in a single statement, "God wanted His people to learn but two things: *holiness* and *justice!*" He wanted them to be clean (to be holy) and to be fair (to be honest). That is why *the corporate Man* with *compounded anointing* must be taught the Word of God above all. But instruction always carries with it the responsibility and accountability to practice what has been taught.

The Church in the wilderness was *kept* during the hour of trial; *delivered* by blood, water, and Spirit; *supernaturally supplied*; and *instructed* in the ways of God. Now would come the most difficult time of all—the time of *sifting*.

Chapter Seven

Four Deadly Sins That Threaten the Corporate Anointing

"But with many of them God was not well pleased...."

1 Corinthians 10:5

Over three million people came out of Egypt under Moses, but *only three* entered the Promised Land, and one of them was dead (Joshua, Caleb, and the bones of Joseph).[1] What happened to the rest of the people?

The answer is vitally important to the Church, the Body of Christ. As God's corporate anointing manifested in the earth, we need to discover why nearly three million people in a "called out nation" died in the wilderness after coming to the very edge of their destiny. I can tell you this much: The problem was that they never made it through the *sifting* that was meant to separate them from their *deadly sins*.

1 Cor. 10:5-10, KJV

But with many of them God was not well pleased: for they were overthrown in the wilderness.

Now these things were our examples, to the intent we should not lust after evil things, as they also lusted.

Neither be ye idolaters, as were some of them; as it is written, The people sat down to eat and drink, and rose up to play.

Neither let us commit fornication, as some of them committed, and fell in one day three and twenty thousand.

Neither let us tempt Christ, as some of them also tempted, and were destroyed of serpents.

Neither murmur ye, as some of them also murmured, and were destroyed of the destroyer.

The Church in the Wilderness Was Sifted in Four Specific Areas

1. Murmuring (Num. 11:1-3).

2. Carnality (Num. 11:4-6).

3. Rebellion (Num. 12; 16–17).

4. Unbelief (Num. 13–14).

The Deadly Sin of Murmuring

Num. 11:1-3, KJV

*And **when the people complained**, it displeased the Lord: and the Lord heard it; and His anger was kindled; and **the fire of the Lord burnt among them**, and consumed them that were in the uttermost parts of the camp.*

And the people cried unto Moses; and when Moses prayed unto the Lord, the fire was quenched.

And he called the name of the place Taberah: because the fire of the Lord burnt among them.

The first thing Jehovah began to sift was *murmuring* and complaining. The Greek word for "murmur" in First Corinthians 10:10 is *gogguzo* and means "to grumble." It also means "to mutter, to say anything in a low tone."[2]

The Hebrew word for "complained" in Numbers 11:1 means "to mourn."[3] The primary Hebrew word for "murmur" is *luwn*, and it means "to stop (usually over night); to stay permanently; hence (in a bad sense) to be obstinate (especially in words, to complain)."[4] (It is translated as "murmur(-ed)" in the King James Version in exactly 13 different verses throughout the Pentateuch—13 is the Bible number denoting *rebellion*).[5] When we murmur, the Lord *always* hears it, and His only recourse is to burn it with fire.[6]

Men murmur because they live on the "uttermost parts"—the edges, borders, or extremities of the camp—far from the presence of God. Get off the back pew and move closer into the courts of the Lord. The tribe of Judah, which means "praise," camped on the east side right by the door. Be a praiser, not a murmurer. When we praise Him, we raise Him. The murmurers were sifted out of the Church of the wilderness and burned with fire. God hasn't changed—will we?

The Deadly Sin of Carnality

Num. 11:4-6, KJV

*And the **mixt multitude** that was among them **fell a lusting:** and the children of Israel also wept again, and said, **Who shall give us flesh** to eat?*

*We remember the fish, which **we did eat in Egypt freely**; the cucumbers, and the melons, and the leeks, and the onions, and the garlick:*

*But **now our soul is dried away**: there is nothing at all, beside this manna, before our eyes.*

Once God shook the Church in the wilderness and sifted out all the murmurers, the next deadly sin to go was *carnality.*

Then as now, there was a "mixt multitude" in the Church. This term means "gathered up together; a *promiscuous* assemblage (of people)."[7] God hates a mixture. Carnal people are ever "lusting." This word means "a longing, a delight." Also rendered as "desire" in the King James Version, its root word means "to wish for."[8]

Israel "wept" or "bemoaned" their situation, and longed for "flesh" and the delicate herbs and spices of their former bondage.[9] The people chose to lust for the memories of the land of bondage. Carnal people cannot let go of the lust of the flesh, the lust of the eyes, and the pride of life—all that is in the world.[10]

Before their deliverance by the blood of the Passover lamb, Israel partook of Egypt's menu "freely" or "gratis, devoid of cost." This word, "freely," in Numbers 11:5 is also translated as "without a cause, to cost nothing."[11] This is deception, for even in days of inflation, the "wages of sin" are still the same (Rom. 6:23)! We will all reap what we sow.[12]

The root word for "dried away" in Numbers 11:6 means "to be ashamed or disappointed."[13] Carnal people are ashamed of the manna, the Word of God. They easily tire of sound Bible preaching and teaching and begin to desire or lust for their cost-free, self-centered lifestyles before Christ.[14] The remainder of Numbers 11 shows how God plagued those who lusted after the flesh of Egypt. He sent them quail until it ran out their noses and ears! Then He buried them in a place called Kibroth-hatta'avah, which means "graves of the longing."[15]

The Deadly Sin of Rebellion

Num. 12:1, KJV

> *And Miriam and Aaron **spake against Moses** because of the Ethiopian woman whom he had married....*

God quickly sifted the Church in the wilderness to filter out the deadly sins of murmuring and carnality. But then a third problem arose with Miriam and Aaron in Numbers 12, and with Korah and his co-conspirators in Numbers 16 and 17—the deadly sin of *rebellion*.

Moses had married Zipporah, an Ethiopian woman and the daughter of Jethro, a descendant of Midian.[16] When God's chosen leader was openly challenged and rebuked by his older siblings, Miriam and Aaron, for his interracial marriage (perhaps they were jealous over the influence of Jethro in Moses' life), Jehovah Himself swiftly came to his defense.

God despises marriages and relationships with *unsaved, idolatrous* mates and companions. An "unequal yoke" in the sight of God refers specifically to His children becoming joined with "unbelievers," *not* to the union of two believers with different skin colors, nationalities, or cultures (2 Cor. 6:14). *The issue is sin, not skin!*[17]

In those biblical incidences where a curse involved *skin color*, it is interesting to see that God turned the offender's skin *white* and not black. Miriam and later Gehazi were smitten with leprosy and their skin became "white as snow" (Num. 12:10; 2 Kings 5:27). When Miriam became so upset with her little brother's dark-skinned African wife that she rebelled against God's authority, His quick response almost seems to be saying, "If you want to see white, *I'll show you white!*"

It is a sobering thought to realize that Miriam *had been mightily anointed* along with her two brothers to liberate a nation.[18] She was disqualified only when she rebelled and got out of her place (not as a woman, but as a child of God) by fearlessly railing against Jehovah's delegated authority in Numbers 12:1. The problem for her *and for us today* is that "the Lord heard it" (Num. 12:2). Rebellion will cause the glory cloud of God's presence to remove from a congregation.[19] Miriam's act of sedition impacted the entire camp, and the entire Church in the wilderness was unable to move forward until Miriam was healed.[20] Rebellion is a deadly sin that cannot be condoned, overlooked, or hidden. It affects the entire corporate anointing.

Num. 16:1-3, KJV

> *Now Korah...took men:*
>
> *And they rose up before Moses...*
>
> *And **they gathered themselves together against Moses** and against Aaron, and said unto them, **Ye take too much upon you**....*

Jude 11, KJV

> *Woe unto them! for they have gone in **the way of Cain**, and ran greedily after **the error of Balaam for reward**, and perished in **the gainsaying of Core** [Korah].*

The offense of Korah and his cronies was one of the most grievous offenses against God that are recorded in the Scriptures. His sin of collective, corporate rebellion is clearly pictured in the three frogs or "unclean spirits" of Revelation 16:13 and revealed in Jude 11 above.

1. *The way of Cain* is the spirit of brother-killing. This spirit works to make men jealous of those whom the Lord has accepted.

2. *The error of Balaam* is the spirit of preaching or prophesying *for reward*—the love of money. These people earn the wages of unrighteousness, living in two worlds with a divided heart. They refuse to obey God's Word instantly, hoping to delay for their own way or gain.

3. *The gainsaying of Core* (or Korah) is the evil spirit inspiring corporate rebellion against God's delegated authority. Miriam and Aaron defied Moses alone, but Korah gathered the leading princes to himself, hoping to win all of the Church of the wilderness to his own cause. Korah had praise in him (pictured by the censer of incense in Numbers 16:6), but he wanted equality and loved to vote. The word for "gainsaying" is *antilogia* and means "dispute, disobedience." It literally means "against or instead of the word." It is also translated in the King James Version as "contradiction, strife," and its root means "to refuse."[21]

Korah, along with Dathan and Abiram and their company of 250 leading princes, were an influential group of ambitious and envious men who blatantly challenged the authority of Moses and attempted to intrude into the priestly office.[22] They accused Moses of that for which they themselves were guilty, and then blamed him for the consequences of their own unbelief.[23] God vindicated His appointed servants and confirmed His chosen priesthood then, and He still does the same thing today!

As always, the rebellious were punished. The glory of the Lord appeared and the ringleaders were swallowed up by an earthquake and sent down alive into Sheol, and fire consumed their 250 followers.[24] The brass censers of the rebels were hammered into broad plates to cover the altar as a memorial to their uprising. Even so, this contagious sin persisted, causing the wrath of God to fall upon 14,700 more of the Israelites! God deals harshly with rebellion in the Church, although in His mercy He always begins His admonishments with His Word today:

Num. 16:26, KJV

> *...Depart, I pray you, from the tents of these wicked men, and touch nothing of theirs, lest ye be consumed in all their sins.*

The Deadly Sin of Unbelief

Murmuring, carnality, and rebellion...

These spiritual enemies of corporate anointing were all sifted out of the Church in the wilderness, but the greatest challenge was the final one. In the end, with the exceptions of Joshua and Caleb (and the bones of faithful Joseph), this deadly sin brought early death and permanent separation from the divine land of promise to every living soul over the age of 20 in that company. That sin was *unbelief*.

Num. 13:20, KJV

> *...Now the time was the time of the firstripe grapes.*

Israel's unbelief at Kadesh-Barnea is the turning point of the Book of Numbers. First, the 12 spies were sent into Canaan at the request of the people (not God).[25] The timing of Israel's arrival is important; it was the time of "firstripe grapes," which is a type of the Feast of Pentecost as well as a foretaste of the fullness of God.[26]

Some people in the modern Church only want to "raid Canaan"—the land of God's fullness and abiding presence—

but twice a year with a "Spring or Fall revival." But why send spies for a quick and short-lived raid when we can *live* in those heavenly places, flowing continuously in compound anointing?[27]

When the spies returned after 40 days (40 denotes testing and trial in the Bible), they brought back the grapes of Eshcol. Eshcol means "cluster" and represents corporate anointing. Numbers 13:26-33 reveals the ten spies' skepticism, and the reaction of the people to their evil report demonstrates the infectious blindness and unreasonableness of unbelief.[28]

In their terminal unbelief, the people looked up at their circumstances with a grasshopper mentality.[29] Caleb and Joshua, on the other hand, beheld the same giants and walled cities as the other spies, but they saw things from the perspective of the heavens. They boldly declared, "They are bread for us" (Num. 14:9), and the people wanted to stone their voices of faith.[30] They should have listened to their two faithful witnesses, but they didn't. *The doubt and unbelief of the children of Israel earned them a death sentence that produced 100 funerals per day for almost 40 years!*

This tragedy and the resulting sin of presumption pictures those in our day who want to stay in the in-part realm of Pentecost, refusing to move on into the corporate fullness of the Feast of Tabernacles.[31] Limited to merely personal or individual anointing, they presume to do battle with the enemy, but are always defeated by the flesh (the Amalekites). Their singular and separated human wisdom and strength are not the way to the top of the hill (Zion). We cannot ascend without the Ark (God's government), or without Moses (the man through whom that government comes to us). And we can never ascend apart.

The Modern Church at the Crossing

The modern Church came to its own Kadesh-Barnea between 1900–1910 A.D. Pentecostals refused to go any further and built their fenced cities between 1910–1920. God's Spirit-filled people came to Kadesh-Barnea *again* in 1948, but once more, the religious Pentecostal tradition prevailed. Perhaps now, years later, "this time around the mountain," some brave, faith-filled Caleb will still the hellish voice of fear and unbelief that bids us die unfulfilled and before our time in the wilderness of our own unbelief. Some will want to stone him, but he will live long enough to take their children in! Can you hear the urgent voice of the Spirit speaking to the Church once again through the word of Caleb?

Num. 13:30, KJV

...Let us go up at once, and possess it; for we are well able to overcome it.

The Third Baptism

Under Moses, the "church in the wilderness" was *kept* during the hour of trial; *delivered* by the blood, the water, and the Spirit; *supernaturally supplied* with bread from Heaven and water from the rock; *instructed* in holiness and justice; and *sifted* in the areas of murmuring, carnality, rebellion, and unbelief.[32]

To carry this story out of the Pentateuch and into the historical books of the Old Testament, we must understand that there is a *third baptism*—not into Moses, but into Joshua!

Deut. 6:23, KJV

*And **He brought us out** from thence, **that He might bring us in**....*

God brought the children of Israel out of Egypt and led them through the wilderness by the hand of *Moses the shepherd.* But He brought them into the land of promise and corporate fulfillment by the word of *Joshua the soldier.*

Both of these leaders, Moses and Joshua, typify Jesus.[33] It's the same Jesus, but the order, administration, and operation of the Spirit has changed. Now we are under commandment because our fullness has come in Christ.[34] Up till now, God did everything *for us* (including putting our breakfast, our manna, on the lawn). But now the manna has ceased and our diet has changed because we have crossed over from wilderness to promise.[35] For the first time in 40 years, we must "prepare victuals" because now we are laborers together with Him.[36]

Moses is dead. It's a new day.[37] In the past, we were content to let the man of God go up the mountain *for us* to hear what the Lord was saying. The problem is that most folks want to party until Moses gets back.[38]

In these New Testament days the veil is rent and *we can all go up the mountain together*! Corporate anointing is far more than everybody "doing what the pastor says." *Compounded anointing will blow everybody out of the bleachers and onto the ball field!* (There are no spectator seats, padded pews, or couches in the House of the compound anointing.)

We have already seen that Israel was baptized into Moses in the Red Sea and the cloud, prefiguring our baptism into Jesus Christ in water and in the Holy Spirit. Now there is a *third baptism* into Joshua at the Jordan River! "Jordan" means "descender" and speaks of complete death to self.[39] This third baptism is a *corporate baptism of fire* that tries every man's work.[40]

There are many who, like the tribes of Reuben, Gad, and the half tribe of Manasseh, will only journey to the borders of corporate destiny, and then refuse to enter in.[41] Take courage, brethren. Keep on praying. This is not the time to faint.[42] Don't draw back; draw near to Jordan with full assurance of faith.[43]

The Day of Atonement, the threshingfloor, the Garden of Gethsemane, the renewing or renovating of the mind, the affliction and consequent transformation of the soul, the ascending of Mount Zion—these are but a few spiritual synonyms for this third baptism.

Next we must explore one more—we will grow up from the unity of the Spirit into the corporate, anointed unity of the faith.

Chapter Eight

Corporate Anointing and Unity

"Behold, how good and how pleasant it is for
brethren to dwell together in *unity*! It is like
the *precious ointment* upon the head...."

Psalm 133:1-2

We have already learned that the anointing is a Person,
and that God's corporate anointing is fully demonstrated on
three progressive levels—it is *poured* out, *smeared* on, and
rubbed in. The Psalmist declared that *unity* is like the corporate anointing!

The fullness of this anointing (or Anointed One) is
clearly modeled in the Tabernacle of Moses and the "church
in the wilderness" (Acts 7:38), whose portrait stretches
across the canvas of the Pentateuch and into the historical
books of the Bible. Now, remember that God begins His
purposes with *a man* (singular) and consummates them in
and through a *people* (plural).

Is. 52:7, KJV

> *How beautiful upon the mountains are **the feet of him** that bringeth good tidings, that publisheth peace; that bringeth good tidings of good, that publisheth salvation; that saith unto Zion, Thy God reigneth!*

Rom. 10:15, KJV

> *And how shall they preach, except they be sent? as it is written, How beautiful are **the feet of them** that preach the gospel of peace, and bring glad tidings of good things!*

Did you notice the transformation made between the Old and New Testaments? The mystery of salvation began with the beautiful feet of *Him* and became the beautiful feet of *them*! The beautiful feet of Jesus the Messiah have become the beautiful feet of the corporate Messiah in the earth, His Body, the Church.[1]

The New Testament term for "beautiful" means "belonging to the right hour or season (timely); flourishing (beauteous)."[2] It describes that which is seasonable, produced at the right time, as of the prime of life, or the time when anything is at its loveliest and best.

The Church's finest hour is just before us! The time to favor Zion, the set time, is come. This is when the Lord will build up Zion (His Church) and appear in that corporate glory.[3]

As you move from the Old Testament to the New Testament, you may notice that the Holy Ghost seems to make everything bigger and "better." The writer of the Book of Hebrews describes this with the Greek word *kreitton*, which means "stronger, nobler."[4] In the eighth chapter he writes, "But now hath He obtained a more excellent ministry, by how much also He is the mediator of a *better* covenant, which was established upon *better* promises" (Heb. 8:6). His feet are multiplied into our feet—"Him" becomes "us"!

Another incredible picture of corporate anointing is found in Psalm 133, the fourteenth of the 15 Songs of Degrees. Often called the "Psalm of Unity," it is the song of one great household, the song of the communion of the saints. It reveals the principles of unity, anointing, and blessing in Zion. This is the psalm of brotherly love and fraternal harmony.

In this psalm, the pilgrims who began their journey in Psalm 120 have at last arrived in the city. In finding Jehovah *they have found each other*! A new social order has been created. It is like the rich oil of experience and the fresh dew, the renewal of all life. The source of this commanded blessing is *God Himself*.

Real Unity Flows Down From the Head

Ps. 133:1-2, KJV

*Behold, how good and how pleasant it is for brethren to dwell together in **unity**!*

*It is **like the precious ointment** upon the head, that ran down upon the beard, even Aaron's beard: that went down to the skirts of his garments.*

It is good and delightful to the Holy Ghost for brethren to "dwell" or "sit down; to marry" in real covenantal commitment. We are to dwell "together" as a "unit," joined and compounded by the art of the apothecary. We must endeavor to keep the "unity of the Spirit" until we come into the "unity of the faith" (Eph. 4:3,13).

The anointing is a Person—the Spirit of the Son who is the Head of the Church. The anointing or ointment (the

Hebrew root is the same for each[5]) is "precious." This word in the Hebrew means "good, favorable, festive, pleasant, pleasing, well, better, right, best."[6]

This precious ointment, the "olive oil" typifying the anointing that rested on Jesus was:

1. Poured on the Rock where Jacob rested (Gen. 28:18).

2. Burned for light (Ex. 25:6).

3. Used to make unleavened bread (Ex. 29:2).

4. Used for cleansing the leper (Lev. 14:17).

5. Used to anoint shield-leather (2 Sam. 1:21).

6. Used to anoint kings (2 Kings 9:6).

7. A sign of outpoured joy (Ps. 23:5).

8. Mingled to make perfume (Song 1:3).

Corporate unity is like the precious oil that ran "down" Aaron's priestly beard. Oil on the beard is a picture of the full-grown priest, the many-membered new creation man in *maturity* and *completeness*. This anointing rushed "down" to the "skirts" or "edges" of his vestments, to the borders of his robes.

Jn. 17:21-23, KJV

*That they **all may be one**; as thou, Father, art in Me, and I in Thee, **that they also may be one in Us:** that the world may believe that Thou hast sent Me.*

And the glory which Thou gavest Me I have given them; that they may be one, even as We are one:

*I in them, and Thou in Me, **that they may be made perfect in one**....*

The word for "perfect" found in our Lord's high priestly prayer in John 17:23 is *teleioo* and means "to complete;

(literally) to accomplish, or (figuratively) to consummate (in character)." It also means "to being to an end, fulfill."[7] It comes from the Greek root word *teleios*, which is translated as "of full age, man, perfect" in the King James Version.[8] This prayer, which is still being answered by the heavenly Father as you read these words, reveals two vital truths of great importance to the Church today.

First, *all true unity essentially flows "down" from the glorious, inter-theistic union of God the Father and God the Son.* You and I have each been given the privilege and the right to fellowship in and with that mystery.[9]

Second, *this corporate unity and anointing will bring healing to others.* The woman with the issue of blood who touched the "border" of Jesus' garment was delivered (Lk. 8:43-44). She pictures the American Church bleeding to death because of the bloody issues that men have raised (for "out of [the heart] are the issues of life," according to Proverbs 4:23).

Our Savior came forth from the bosom of the Father— now Jesus is the issue![10] Once the woman pressed through all that other stuff and touched Him and His anointing, she was set free! The Church is pressing through its mess this very moment, lunging for His garments of wholeness.[11]

Ps. 133:3, KJV

As the dew of Hermon, and as the dew that descended upon the mountains of Zion: for there the Lord commanded the blessing, even life for evermore.

Dew is a rich symbol of the blessing of the Holy Spirit and the unity He brings.[12] The fountainhead for the oil was the head of Aaron. The dew "descended" from off Hermon (the ancient name for Mount Zion).

It was there—and *only there*—in the place of corporate unity and anointing, that the Lord has "commanded" or "ordered" blessing, benediction, and prosperity: ever-increasing, abundant, overflowing life![13] This is the place and ordained blessing of our destiny.

Practical Dynamics of Unity

Real unity cannot be created, because men have tried and failed. It can only be kept.[14] Unity flows downward to us from the relationship between the Father and the Son, and it is based upon the seven absolutes of Ephesians 4:4-6. For example, the fact that He is your Lord and my Lord makes us one.

We must preach, teach, and demonstrate the unity of the Body of Christ in all that we do. The household of faith is one family, and spiritual brothers and sisters who do their Father's will have a stronger tie than natural kinfolk![15] A house divided against itself cannot stand; it will become "desolate" or "laid waste," and the House of God is *not* exempt.[16] According to John the apostle, if we do not love our brother, the love of God is not in us.[17] Jesus said even our sacrifices, offerings, and prayers are no good if we have built walls between each other.[18] In fact, Jesus named *only one thing* that would show the world that His Church was of God:

Jn. 13:35, KJV

> **By this** shall all men **know that ye are My disciples**, *if ye have* **love one to another**.

Jesus is our peace, our bond of unity and harmony.[19] He made one in Himself of all races, nations, classes, and genders who have received Him. His finished work rent the veil separating man from God and broke down the hostile dividing wall between brethren.

Now, out of jealousy and envy, we have constructed *new walls* with our various beliefs and interpretations of the Scriptures.[20] This often joins with greed to create division, and such traditions of men have nullified His Word.[21] When complacency and pride are added to this witches' brew, there's "nothing but death in that pot."[22]

Christians who do not love one another make a blanket statement to the world that they are not real. The Church cannot receive God's fullest blessings until we together walk in love and agreement as individual members of His Body and lift up Jesus.[23] Love means preferring your brother above yourself, and it hits the devil where it hurts the most. Love binds us together and preserves us as a supernatural family.[24]

Rom. 12:4-5, KJV

For as we have many members in one body, and all members have not the same office:

*So **we, being many, are one body in Christ,** and **every one members one of another**.*

The apostle Paul went on in Romans 12 to mention several gifts and ministries (a divine apothecary) that God has given various members of the Body to help "put us together" and teach us to operate in the will of the Holy Spirit.

Eph. 4:11-13, KJV

And He gave some, apostles; and some, prophets; and some, evangelists; and some, pastors and teachers;

*For the **perfecting** of the saints, **for the work of the ministry**, for the **edifying** of the body of Christ:*

***Till** we all **come in the unity of the faith,** and of the knowledge of the Son of God, **unto a perfect man**, unto the measure of the stature of the fulness of Christ.*

Paul also listed the ascension-gift ministries (extensions of Jesus Himself) sent forth into the Body of Christ to mature the saints and equip them to do the work of the ministry.[25]

Since unity indicates spiritual maturity, we must learn to discern the "good" of loving the brethren and the "evil" of division and dissension because God hates those who sow discord among brethren.[26] The mark of spiritual maturity is discernment. We must ever be "discerning" of the Body, knowing that when we offend one of the least of His brethren, we violate Him![27]

All His promises are for the *universal* Church; therefore, we cannot receive God's blessings while separated from the rest of the Body. As individuals, we can only participate in the promises and privileges of sonship by becoming and remaining an active, lively member of the *corporate Man*, working for its overall fulfillment.[28]

Unity brings blessing, and blessing brings the glory of God. For there to be unity in the Body of Christ, there must first be unity in the home between the husband and the wife and between parents and children. On a larger scale, the only way to have unity between races and nations is for there to be unity in the Church. *As the Church goes, so goes the world.* That is why Jesus commanded us to be *salt* and *light*.[29]

Lev. 26:8, KJV

And five of you shall chase an hundred, and an hundred of you shall put ten thousand to flight: and your enemies shall fall before you by the sword.

The Prayers of Jesus Are Answered

The final prayer Jesus prayed before His death *was for the unity of His disciples* in John 17:20-24. Now He "ever liveth to make intercession for [us]" (Heb. 7:25).[30] That clearly demonstrates His position on the issue of unity!

Christ in us *is* the hope of glory—His own hope.[31] Jesus is God, and God only has faith in Himself. That means *His* prayers will be *answered*!

Ps. 72:20, KJV

The prayers of David the son of Jesse are ended.

Three Old Testament men typify Jesus Christ more than any others: Adam, Abraham, and David.[32] In Adam, we see the *pain* of the Seed of the woman who relates to mankind *racially*; that is, the Word was made flesh. In Abraham, we behold the *promise* of the Seed of Abraham who relates to us *redemptively*. But it is in David that we see the *power* of our King, the greatest Seed of David, who relates to His people *royally*.

Psalm 72 is "A Psalm for (pertaining to) Solomon." This is a great Kingdom psalm, describing the exalted King and the blessing of His global reign over all nations.[33] This is a prayer *for* the king *by a king*. The Feast of Tabernacles is detailed throughout all 20 verses, and it prophetically paints a Messianic picture of what the earth will look like under the Lordship of Jesus Christ.[34] This is a great "theocratic" psalm because the whole perfect order of the *rule and government of God* is revealed as He is high over all and enthroned, actively governing the affairs of men and nations and every created thing.

David is a type of Jesus Christ, and Solomon prefigures His seed—the overcoming, glorious Church. Every verse of this psalm is applicable to King Jesus, whose rule and reign is consummated through His Body, the corporate Man, with manifold grace and anointing.

First, it is important to view the psalms, including Psalm 72, as the "prayers" of David. King David ends Psalm 72 by saying, "The *prayers* of David...are ended" (Ps. 72:20).[35]

Second, note that these prayers of David are "ended." This word in the Hebrew is *kalah*, and it means "to end (cease, finish) or *complete*."[36] Jesus' prayers will accomplish their purpose. In John 17, He prayed that a corporate anointing would make us to become one, even as He and the Father are one, and Ephesians 4:1-16 spells out the details of that fulfillment.

The King declared that He would personally "build" or "construct" His Church, and His commitment stands for something.[37] When He decrees a thing, it happens. If every television or radio station in the world stopped carrying Christian programming, and if every publication, book, or Bible were taken away, Jesus would *still build His Church*. Jesus' prayers will be answered!

Jn. 17:22, KJV

> And **the glory which Thou gavest Me** I *have given them;* **that they may be one**, *even as We are one.*

Know this: Glory is unity, and unity is glory! Unity releases glory. The glorious Church is a unified Church, where everything is gathered unto Him.

The opposite to this one vision is "di-vision" or two visions. This crippling double-mindedness can operate in a person, home, church, community, or nation. When that happens, we cannot walk with Him.[38] But the day will come when the whole earth will be filled with the glory—and therefore the unity—of the Lord![39]

Having discussed *compounded anointing* and Jesus' objective of unity, we now turn our attention toward another vital aspect of our call—corporate anointing and the name of God. The Scriptures tell us that *His name* is "as *ointment* poured forth..." (Song 1:3).

Chapter Nine

Corporate Anointing and the Name of God

"…thy name is as ointment poured forth…."

Song of Solomon 1:3

The Person of Jesus Christ is the genesis of all anointing, revealed in three dimensions.[1] Real unity flows down from our glorious Head to scent the priestly garments that cover His Body, the Church. We've already studied the corporate anointing and the unity of the Spirit that will ultimately bring us all together into the unity of the faith.[2] We are about to explore the thought that anointed unity and glory actually crosses time and the generations of mankind, but first we must understand that compound anointing is directly linked to *the name(s) of God.*

Thy Name Is as Ointment Poured Forth

As we learned earlier, the Song of Songs is an anthem or love song for the Holy of Holies.[3] That His "love is better than wine" (Song 1:2) reveals the surpassing glory of the Most Holy Place where His presence dwells. This is the third dimension of full maturity, the realm *beyond* Pentecost. The wine of the Spirit is the "earnest" or first valuable investment of mature love. The throne room of Revelation 4:3, with its emerald-like rainbow, corresponds to the bedroom of Song of Solomon 1:16—"green" is the biblical color denoting resurrection life. In spite of our odd prudishness at times, God persists in using the most intimate of human relationships to illustrate the eternal union of Father and Son, and of God and man.

Song 1:3, KJV

> *Because of the* **savour** *of thy* **good ointments** *thy* **name** *is as* **ointment poured forth**....

The word "savour" comes from the Hebrew word *rey-ach*, and it means "odor (as if blown)."[4] Its root in noun form is *ruach*, the Hebrew word for "wind, spirit, breath" (compare the Greek word *pneuma*). *Reyach* is also translated as "scent, smell" in the King James Version.[5]

This is an Old Testament picture of the Holy Spirit (*Ruach*) revealing Jesus, the Son. That is the Spirit's great purpose and mission in the earth. Jesus' good "ointments," His *anointing* from the beaten olive oil, is *activated and released by the Spirit*. Jesus was anointed and enabled by the Holy Spirit to *pour out* and empty Himself.[6] (By the way, the long tense in Hebrew is used for "poured forth" in this passage from the Song of Solomon. It denotes a *continual* action. The name of Jesus is "as ointment continually, constantly, even now being poured out" upon us!)

Thou Shalt Call His Name "Jesus"

Mt. 1:21-23, KJV

> *...thou shalt* **call His name JESUS**: *for He shall save His people from their sins.*

Now all this was done, that it might be fulfilled which was spoken of the Lord by the prophet, saying,

*Behold, a virgin shall be with child, and shall bring forth a son, and they shall **call His name Emmanuel**, which being interpreted is, **God with us**.*

Acts 4:12, KJV

*Neither is there salvation in any other: for **there is none other name** under heaven given among men, whereby we must be saved.*

Phil. 2:9, KJV

*Wherefore God also hath highly exalted Him, and **given Him a name** which is **above every name**.*

Throughout the Scriptures, one's name identifies his nature. The name of God reveals all that He is, all that He has, and all that He does. By divine design, every name of God in the Bible finds its consummate fulfillment in the Person and work of the Lord Jesus Christ, the name that is higher than any other.

The Great Commission recorded in Matthew 28:18-20 commands us to baptize the nations in the "name" of the Father, and the Son, and the Holy Ghost. "Father," "Son," and "Holy Ghost" are not names; they are titles. The "name" of the Father, Jehovah God, is given over 7,000 times in the Old Testament, and is translated as "Lord." The name of the Son is "Jesus." Based on the truths we've already examined concerning the "Christ" who never left this planet, the name of the Holy Ghost is "Christ" as the "Spirit of the Son" and the "*Christos*," or the Anointing or Anointed One.

Given these detailed understandings, the three-part name of the "Lord Jesus Christ" is the name of the one triune God. This full name reflects the truth in Paul's statement that in Jesus *dwelt all the fullness* of the *Godhead* bodily.[7] (Does this do away with the triune nature of God? Absolutely not. Does it magnify and lift Jesus higher? Absolutely so.)

Acts 2:38, KJV

...Repent, and be baptized every one of you in the name of Jesus Christ for the remission of sins, and ye shall receive the gift of the Holy Ghost.

Immersion in water into *the name of the Lord Jesus Christ* is the first sealing of the New Covenant whereby our sins are remitted and our hearts are circumcised.[8] It is a public declaration that we have died to sin and have arisen to walk in newness of life *married to a heavenly other*. As with marriage, we have received "the name of our Husband," and two have become one.

You received *His name* in baptism. You have *put on Christ*.[9] Now walk worthy of that calling. Do not take His name in vain.[10]

The "El" Names

Solomon wrote prophetically of the Divine Bridegroom, "Thy name is as ointment poured forth" (Song 1:3). This ointment or anointing was compounded. His compounded name is like compounded oil. We can barely touch on the glorious meaning of each of the compounded "El" and "Jehovah" names of God here within the limited confines of this book. Nevertheless, we must try, for *name denotes nature*. According to God's Word, each of these wonderful names finds its complete expression in Jesus Christ and His glorious Body, revealing a unique aspect of this manifold, corporate anointing that we have received.

Ex. 15:2, KJV

*The Lord is my strength and song, and He is become my salvation: He is **my God**....*

The word for "God" here is *'El,* and it means "strength; mighty; especially the Almighty."[11] "El" finds its perfect fulfillment in the strength and power of the Lamb Christ Jesus, the One who is mighty to save.[12]

The name "El" is the revelation of corporate strength.

Paul knew that He could do all things through "Christ" who strengthened him (Phil. 4:13). He explained this to be the personal, indwelling supply of Christ, as well as the corporate Christ who lived and worked through the prayers of the saints in behalf of his deliverance.[13]

Gen. 1:1, KJV

*In the beginning **God created** the heaven and the earth.*

The name of the Creator God in the first five chapters of the Book of Genesis is "Elohim." The Hebrew word is *'elohiym* and it means "gods in the ordinary sense; but specifically used (*in the plural* thus, *especially with the article*) of *the supreme God.*"[14] "Elohim" is the plural of *'Eloah* (a prolonged form of *'el*), which means "a deity or the Deity."[15]

"Elohim" finds its perfect fulfillment in Jesus Christ, for "*all things were made by Him*; and without Him was not any thing made that was made" (Jn. 1:3).[16]

The name "Elohim" is the revelation of corporate creativity.

Each member of the Body of Christ is a unique expression of Him, but the fullness of corporate strength and collective wisdom is found in the *many-membered Christ.*[17] When we pool our efforts in the home and the local church, we can, as a supernatural *team*, mingle the gifts and talents of our individual members and benefit from our corporate strength. In the midst of all of us is the answer to any given situation through the corporate anointing and wisdom of God.

Gen. 17:1, KJV

*...I am the **Almighty God**; walk before Me, and be thou perfect.*

The God who revealed Himself to 90-year-old Abram was "El-Shaddai." This Hebrew word is a compound of *'El* (which we've already studied), and *Shadday*, which means "the Almighty."[18] It comes from the root word *shadad*, which means "powerful, burly."[19] Because of the similarity of this word to the Hebrew root *shad*, or "breast," many translators say *El-Shaddai* means the "breasted one," or the "all-sufficient one," revealing the feminine side of God's nature.[20]

"El-Shaddai" finds its perfect fulfillment in the mercy and compassion of the Lord Jesus. He is our "propitiation" or "mercy-seat" (Rom. 3:25). The Good Shepherd of John 10 is also the Good Samaritan of Luke 10, the One with all "compassion" (Lk. 10:33).[21]

The name "El-Shaddai" is the revelation of corporate mercy and compassion.

God lives in a "three-room House." The third room, the Most Holy Place, is the *living room* and the *loving room*.[22] There is only one piece of furniture in God's living room: the love-seat, the mercy-seat. The Body of Christ is, above all, to be marked by God's love and mercy.[23] That is the only way that the world will know that we are real.[24]

Gen. 14:18-19, KJV

*And Melchizedek king of Salem brought forth bread and wine: and he was the priest of **the most high God**.*

And he blessed him, and said, Blessed be Abram of the most high God, possessor of heaven and earth.

This is perhaps the most lofty of the divine names we have been given in the Old Testament. The "most high God" is "El-Elyon." This is a compound of the Hebrew words *'El* and *'elyown*.[25] The latter term means "an elevation, lofty; as title, the Supreme." It is taken from the primitive root *'alah*, which means "to ascend, be high, or mount."[26] It is significant that this name is closely linked to a similar word, *'olah*, the word for "burnt offering" or "*ascending offering*."[27] "El-Elyon" is translated in the King James Version as "Most high, on high, and upper-most."

"El-Elyon" finds its perfect fulfillment in Jesus Christ, the "Son of the Highest" (Lk. 1:32). He is our great King-Priest after the order, manner, and similitude of Melchisedec.[28] Jesus was the *whole burnt Offering* totally sacrificed for us, and to Him was given all executive authority in Heaven and in earth.[29]

The name "El-Elyon" is the revelation of corporate dominion.

This is in perfect alignment with *God's original intent* to create male and female man "in His image and likeness" and to give them *dominion* over the earth (Gen. 1:26-28). The most high saints of the Most Holy Place who become *a whole burnt offering* will rule and reign with Him.[30] Corporate, not personal, anointing (the anointing of the Head and the Body in ascending union) will be necessary to conquer death, the last enemy.

Chapter Ten

Corporate Anointing and the Redemptive "Jehovah" Names of God

"...thy name is as ointment poured forth...."

Song of Solomon 1:3

Anyone who conducts a thorough study of the compound redemptive names of Jehovah in the Old Testament will discover the unfolding glories of the *covenantal names of God.* Each of these names relate closely to man's needs, and they find their ultimate and complete fulfillment in the *greatest compound redemptive name ever revealed.* This name is unveiled in the New Testament: the Lord Jesus Christ! All the redemptive names of God find their consummation and fullest expression in the living Redeemer Himself.

Gen. 12:1, KJV

*Now the **Lord** had said unto Abram, Get thee out....*

The sacred Hebrew word *Yehovah* (often spelled "Jehovah") is translated as "Lord" in the King James Version more than 7,000 times in the Old Testament.[1] It means "(the) self-Existent or Eternal; Jehovah, Jewish national name of God." It is taken from the Hebrew root word *hayah*, which means "to exist; to be or become."[2]

When Jehovah revealed His name to Moses, He declared it to be "I AM THAT I AM" (Ex. 3:14-15). This could be translated, "*I shall be there* [His person] as *who I am* [His power] *shall I be there* [His promise]." Another rendering of "Jehovah" is "*I am, I was, I will be.*"

"Jehovah" finds its complete fulfillment in Jesus Christ, whom the Bible calls the "express image" and "brightness of [the Father's] glory" (Heb. 1:3). Jesus of Nazareth was God Almighty, the "I AM" in the flesh, the eternal, self-existent Word who came forth from the Father's bosom.[3] Jesus declared, "Lo, *I am* with you alway" (Mt. 28:20). He is "Alpha and Omega" (Rev. 1:11). Jesus knew exactly what He was doing each and every time He spoke the Eternal Name of "I Am" and openly claimed it as His own.[4] This was especially true of His bold declaration in John 8:58: "Jesus said unto them, Verily, verily, I say unto you, *Before* Abraham was, *I am.*"

The name "Jehovah" is the revelation of corporate covenantal constancy.

Jehovah is the covenant God, and we are His covenant people. He abides with us, and we abide with Him and with one another. Covenant is marked by faithfulness.[5] Those who follow the Lamb are called, chosen, and faithful.[6] Those who are faithful unto death will be given the crown of life.[7] Drawing from God's revelation to Moses, Paul declared, "But by the grace of God I am what I am..." (1 Cor. 15:10).

Gen. 22:14, KJV

And Abraham called the name of that place
Jehovah-jireh: *as it is said to this day, In the mount
of the Lord it shall be seen.*

"Jehovah-Jireh" means "the Lord will see and provide."
It is a compound of *Jehovah* and *Yir'eh*, which means
"Jehovah will see (to it); Jehovah-Jireh, a symbolical name
for Mount Moriah."[8] It can also mean "the Lord will behold,
Jehovah will provide."

"Jehovah-Jireh" finds its perfect fulfillment in Jesus
Christ, the One who meets our every need.[9] He is the sub-
stitutionary Ram caught in the thicket of our sins and
offered in our rightful place.[10]

*The redemptive name "Jehovah-Jireh" is the revelation
of corporate provision.*

As brothers and sisters in the same family, we must
depend upon one another. Everything we need is found in His
Body. We are members one of another, and we must ever pray
for each other, seeing the need and meeting the need.[11]

Ex. 15:26, KJV

*And said, If thou wilt diligently hearken to the
voice of the Lord thy God, and wilt do that which is
right in His sight, and wilt give ear to His commandments, and keep all His statutes, I will put none of
these diseases upon thee, which I have brought upon
the Egyptians: for I am* **the Lord that healeth thee**.

"Jehovah-Rapha" means "the Lord who heals." It is a
compound of *Jehovah* and *rapha',* which means "to mend
(by stitching); to cure." It can also mean "to heal, to restore
to normal."[12]

"Jehovah-Rapha" finds its perfect fulfillment in Jesus Christ, our Healer. Jesus came to bring abundant life,[13] and to heal mankind in spirit, soul, and body.[14] God's Word unequivocally declares in *both* Testaments, "By His stripes we were healed" (Is. 53:5; 1 Pet. 2:24).

The redemptive name "Jehovah-Rapha" is the revelation of corporate healing.

James declared, "Confess your faults one to another, and pray one for another, that ye may be healed" (Jas. 5:16a). Through the spoken word and the laying on of hands, we have all been commissioned to minister healing to others.[15]

Ex. 17:15, KJV

> *And Moses built an altar, and called the name of it **Jehovah-nissi**.*

"Jehovah-Nissi" means "the Lord our banner." It is a compound of *Jehovah* and *nec,* which means "banner; flag; sail; flagstaff; signet; token." Its root means "to gleam from afar; to lift up as an ensign." The full name can also mean "Jehovah is my high standard; Jehovah is my conspicuous sign."[16]

"Jehovah-Nissi" finds its perfect fulfillment in mankind's only Savior who was lifted up on the wooden altar of His cross.[17] It was there that Heaven's Standard-bearer was completely victorious over sin, sickness, poverty, and death.[18]

The redemptive name "Jehovah-Nissi" is the revelation of corporate victory.

As we lift up one another's hands in the strength of the Lord, the flesh (typified by Amalek) is subdued.[19] To walk alone is asking for defeat. Together, we are a victorious people who walk by faith, knowing that the war has been won.[20] His triumph is the basis of all our worship, symbolized by Moses' altar.

Ex. 31:13, KJV

*Speak thou also unto the children of Israel, saying, Verily My sabbaths ye shall keep: for it is a sign between Me and you throughout your generations; that ye may know that I am **the Lord that doth sanctify you**.*

"Jehovah-Makaddesh" means "the Lord who sanctifies." It is a compound of *Jehovah* and *qadash*, which means "to be (make, pronounce, observe as) clean (ceremonially or morally)." It means "to be holy, to sanctify."[21] To "sanctify" is to set apart a person or thing unto the Lord for exclusively holy purposes.

"Jehovah-Makaddesh" finds its perfect fulfillment in Jesus Christ, who is made unto us "sanctification" (1 Cor. 1:30). When His side was pierced on Calvary, there came out blood and water for our cleansing.[22] Jesus is the holy, harmless, spotless, sinless Son of God, the perfect sacrifice.[23]

The redemptive name "Jehovah-Makaddesh" is the revelation of corporate holiness.

The many-membered new creation Man is "created in righteousness and true holiness" (Eph. 4:24). Together, we comprise a "holy nation" that was sanctified by blood from birth (1 Pet. 2:9). It is our responsibility to sanctify ourselves individually and corporately by the washing of water by the Word.[24] There remains a *sabbath rest* for the "people" of God (Heb. 4:9) under the New Covenant, and it is imperative that we be a covenant people who keep His sabbath rest.[25]

Judg. 6:24, KJV

*Then Gideon built an altar there unto the Lord, and called it **Jehovah-shalom**: unto this day it is yet in Ophrah of the Abi-ezrites.*

"Jehovah-Shalom" means "the Lord our peace." It is a compound of *Jehovah* and *shalowm*, which means "safe, well, happy, friendly; also welfare, health, prosperity, peace." Its root means "to be safe (in mind, body, or estate), to be (make) completed."[26] It can also mean "Jehovah is perfection, Jehovah is completely finished, Jehovah is friendliness, Jehovah is prosperity."

"Jehovah-Shalom" finds its perfect fulfillment in the One who literally and personally "is our peace" (Eph. 2:14). Jesus Christ is the Prince of peace, the King of peace, and the Benefactor and divine Administrator of peace, but His peace is "not as the world giveth" (Jn. 14:27).[27] Jesus made peace with all men through the blood of His cross.[28]

The redemptive name "Jehovah-Shalom" is the revelation of corporate peace.

Believers have peace *with* God and the peace *of* God according to Romans 5:1. Now we can truly worship God (as pictured in Gideon's altar). The Kingdom that we share is marked by righteousness, peace, and joy in the Holy Ghost.[29] To be carnally (individually) minded is death; to be spiritually (corporately) minded is life and peace.[30] We are to keep the unity of the Spirit in the bond of peace, for then the God of peace will quickly bruise satan under our corporate feet.[31]

Judg. 11:27, KJV

*Wherefore I have not sinned against thee, but thou doest me wrong to war against me: **the Lord the Judge** be judge this day between the children of Israel and the children of Ammon.*

"Jehovah-Shaphat" means "the Lord our judge." It is a compound of *Jehovah* and *shaphat*, which means "to judge; to pronounce sentence (for or against); to vindicate or punish; to govern; to litigate." It can also mean "to deliver, rule."[32]

"Jehovah-Shaphat" finds its perfect fulfillment in the One who is both Savior and righteous Judge.[33] His Spirit, the Holy Spirit, has been sent to convict men concerning sin, righteousness, and judgment,[34] and to proclaim and reveal Jesus as Governor and King.[35]

The redemptive name "Jehovah-Shaphat" is the revelation of corporate judgment.

The glorious Church, the Body of Christ, will judge the world and judge angels as well.[36] Jesus showed us how to judge righteously,[37] but first and foremost we are to examine ourselves.[38] To help us fulfill this redemptive function of righteous judgment in the earth as the Body of Christ, God has given us corporately the gift of discerning of spirits.[39] In Christ, we are a corporate company of ruling kings and priests.[40]

Jer. 23:6, KJV

In his days Judah shall be saved, and Israel shall dwell safely: and this is His name whereby He shall be called, **THE LORD OUR RIGHTEOUSNESS**.

"Jehovah-Tsidkenu" means "the Lord our righteousness." It is a compound of *Jehovah* and *tsedeq*, which means "the right (natural, moral, or legal); also equity or prosperity."[41]

"Jehovah-Tsidkenu" finds its perfect fulfillment in the One who has been made unto us "righteousness" (1 Cor. 1:30). The Son is the "Sun of righteousness" (Mal. 4:2), and the very scepter of His Kingdom is righteousness.[42] His divine nature is the fruit of the Spirit "in all goodness and *righteousness* and truth" (Eph. 5:9).

The redemptive name "Jehovah-Tsidkenu" is the revelation of corporate righteousness.

Together, we have been made the righteousness of God in Christ.[43] The New Covenant that we all share is the "ministration of righteousness" (2 Cor. 3:9). According to the writings of Paul, as good soldiers, we have put on "the breastplate of righteousness" (Eph. 6:14).[44]

Ps. 23:1, KJV

*The **Lord is my shepherd**; I shall not want.*

Many people don't realize that this beloved Psalm contains one of the great redemptive, covenantal names of God, "Jehovah-Rohi," which means "the Lord our shepherd." It is a compound of *Jehovah* and *ra'ah*, which literally means "to tend a flock; pasture it; to graze; generally to rule; by extension, to associate with (as a friend)."[45] It is also translated as "companion, pastor, shepherd" in the King James Version.

"Jehovah-Rohi" finds its perfect fulfillment in Him who is our good Shepherd, great Shepherd, and chief Shepherd.[46] The prophet Isaiah foresaw the Messiah as a caring Shepherd, and we can safely and securely cast all our care upon Him, because He cares for us.[47]

The redemptive name "Jehovah-Rohi" is the revelation of corporate care.

The Body of Christ is a holy flock, with only one Shepherd and one sheepfold.[48] We are His people, the sheep of His pasture.[49] His Body is to collectively have the *same care* one for the other.[50] One of the five members of the servant dream team that has been sent to mature and equip the saints is the shepherd, or pastor.[51]

Ps. 95:6, KJV

*O come, let us worship and bow down: let us kneel before **the Lord our maker**.*

"Jehovah-Hosenu" means "the Lord our maker." It is a compound of *Jehovah* and *'asah*, which means "to do or make."[52] Every created being, whether man or angel, will one day bow down to Jehovah-Hosenu. The original Hebrew term means "to bend the knee, to sink, to prostrate."

Every creature will also "kneel" before Him, or "bless God as an act of adoration."[53]

"Jehovah-Hosenu" finds its perfect fulfillment in Jesus Christ, the *consummate Worshiper* who ever delighted to please the Father.[54] The great Servant of Jehovah knelt before His Father in total humility and obedience.[55] Jesus was and is the Lamb who receives all blessing and honor.[56]

The redemptive name "Jehovah-Hosenu" is the revelation of corporate worship and humility.

All of us are to worship God in spirit and in truth as *true worshipers*.[57] We are to have the mind of Christ, the mind of a humble servant.[58] In meekness, we are to prefer one another, humbling ourselves under His mighty "hand" (1 Pet. 5:5-6).[59] As we stated earlier, *every knee in Heaven and earth* will collectively bow to the name of Jesus.[60]

Ezek. 48:35, KJV

> *It was round about eighteen thousand measures: and **the name of the city** from that day shall be, **The Lord is there***.

The name for God who lived in Ezekiel's Temple was "Jehovah-Shammah"—"the Lord is there." It is a compound of *Jehovah* and *sham*, which means "there." It can also mean "Jehovah is high, Jehovah designates, Jehovah is the great name."[61]

"Jehovah-Shammah" finds its perfect fulfillment in Jesus Christ, the "Lord of glory," who was all the fullness of the Godhead bodily.[62] He was the House that the Father lived in, the living Word who tabernacled among men and was filled and crowned with all the Father's glory and brightness.[63] Jesus has bestowed *that same glory* upon His Church![64]

The redemptive name "Jehovah-Shammah" is the revelation of corporate glory.

Compounded together, the end-time, glorious Church comprises *the fullness of Him* who was the fullness of the Godhead bodily. The Word declares that we are the Church, "which is His body, the fulness of Him that filleth all in all" (Eph. 1:23). The glory of the latter House shall be greater than any other.[65] Together, we are being changed from glory to glory.[66] Christ *in and among each of us* and *all* of us is *the hope of glory*.[67] Remember, *unity is glory*.

Eph. 3:10, KJV

> ...the **manifold wisdom** of God.

1 Pet. 4:10, KJV

> ...the **manifold grace** of God.

As the rainbow-colored covenantal coat of the patriarch Joseph had many folds,[68] so each of the covenantal names of God has revealed the multifaceted nature of compounded anointing. The word for "manifold" in Ephesians 3:10 is *polupoikilos* and means "much variegated, multifarious."[69] *Poikilos*, the word translated as "manifold" in First Peter 4:10, means "motley, various in character."[70] Corporate anointing manifests corporate wisdom and grace.

The Greek word for our "inheritance" is *kleronomia*. It is taken from *kleros* ("lot, allotment, portion, heritage") and *nomos*, transliterated as "name."[71] God has allotted and distributed His anointed name among us.[72]

His name is Jesus, and His name is as *ointment poured forth*. We have become partakers of His divine nature and have taken His name as our own.[73] The "El" and "Jehovah" names of God vividly describe the true nature and multifaceted ministry of the end-time Body of Christ. Our next discovery will be that the glorious, corporate Man, the Church, is receiving the generational anointing of the ages, transcending time and space.

Chapter Eleven

Corporate Anointing Transcends Time and Space

"...the whole family in heaven and earth...."

Ephesians 3:15

In the final two chapters of this book, you and I will discuss how to apply everything that we have learned about *corporate anointing*. This chapter is prophetic and will hang you in the heavens if you have spiritual ears to hear and eyes to see. The last chapter that follows this one is the most practical of all, however, and will bring you safely "back down to earth" and into God's blessing if you remain a doer of the Word.

The truths about to be set before you are meat and not milk. There is a possibility that you will not understand the generational aspect of corporate anointing the first time you hear it, but it is one of the great truths of our eternal Creator's workings with mankind. As I pen these words, I am especially thinking of that special breed of believer who has been "apprehended" for the high calling in Christ (Phil. 3:12-14). I could well have titled this chapter "The Price of Corporate Anointing," but I was concerned that no one would read it. Perhaps our Lord had the same problem when He talked of "counting the cost" (Lk. 14:28). In any case, I rejoice that you are still with me and are determined to finish the course!

Somebody Prayed for You

Every one of us was birthed by *someone else's travail.*[1] Somebody prayed for your salvation because you cannot give birth to yourself.

My dad's aunt, Velma Varner, lived in Davis, West Virginia. She wore her long hair in a neat little bun, played the guitar, and sang praises to Jesus in the Davis Church of God. She was a great cook and a gracious hostess.

As a five-year-old, I remember going to see Aunt Velma and Uncle Paul at their house in Davis. I can still remember sitting in front of their black-and-white television set and watching a man by the name of Oral Roberts boldly praying for the sick. For some reason, that memory was burned into my being and remains there to this day. In later years, I was a music major in college. Again, I have often wondered if my leanings toward music had any connection to my early attempts to play Aunt Velma's old-timey pump organ with all its stops out on her enclosed front porch.

Today I am deeply aware that I am a freak of sovereign grace. I am an outrageous composite of every godly man and woman who ever prayed for me, especially through the laying on of their hands. Deep in my spirit, *I believe that Velma Varner was one of those who prayed* little Teddy (my nickname then) into the Kingdom and into the ministry I have today!

Think about it. Who prayed for you?

Was it your mother, your father, your grandmother, your grandfather, some old preacher, a Sunday school teacher...?

Somebody travailed until you were born from above. Granted, many of those folks are in Heaven, but they are not dead. When we think about them, they are here. *Their anointing* (*chrisma*) *never left the planet*, and I'll tell you why.

When you hear Kelley Varner preach or read the books he has written, *you will also hear the voices and taste the anointing of* A.C. Wilson, George McDowell, G.C. McCurry, Jack Harris, C.S. Fowler, J.L. Dutton, George Hawtin, Bill Britton, George Warnock, Dick Iverson, Kevin Conner, Violet Kitely, J. Preston Eby, Bennie Skinner, "Doc" Agan, Ray Prinzing, Earl Paulk, Mel Bailey, Tommy Reid, Mark Hanby, Clarice Fluitt, Stephen Everett, and many others!

There is a divine plan for each of our lives—our own personal purpose and destiny. And part of our destiny is to be supernaturally *mingled* into His master blueprint, a blueprint that includes *every anointed person who ever touched our lives* (and every person who touched them before they touched us!). Though dead, those righteous ones are yet speaking.[2]

God created time for His own purposes, but that doesn't mean He has *ever* been confined to it or limited by it! Time is measured. The anointing upon Jesus was "without measure" (Jn. 3:34), transcending time! Look closely at what God told Moses, "This shall be *an holy anointing oil* unto Me *throughout your generations*" (Ex. 30:31b). In other words, corporate anointing is generational. It reaches back into the past, gathering up every bit of corporate anointing from those who went before us. It stretches itself out into the future to supernaturally taste the powers of the age to come! Beyond that, it transcends time and space! (This is perfectly pictured in the ultimate *Chrisma*, Jesus Christ, who "was" before Abraham was even born, according to John 8:58. He was "the Lamb slain *from the foundation of the world*" in Revelation 13:8.)

We have arrived at the apex of the ages wherein the Father has begun to head up in Christ all things in Heaven and on earth.[3] When Jesus died on the cross, the earth convulsed and shook at the thought of holding its Creator. Now He is shaking everything.[4] "Tribulation" means "pressure," and we are all under the influence of the pressure of the ages—God is birthing a corporate people in the image of the Pattern Son.[5]

Sovereign Confinement

There is a company of overcomers in the earth who have already been baptized into Moses in the cloud and the sea.[6] The hand of the shepherd brought us out of Egypt and through our adolescent wilderness. But Moses is dead. Now Lord Joshua is our Commander. His word alone is bringing us into the land. We are part of a team of priests who are upholding the Ark of the Covenant of the Lord God of the whole earth. Presently, we are standing in the midst of Jordan in the days of harvest, holding back death until the rest of the nation crosses safely.

We are hated by some and misunderstood by most. As with Nehemiah, it's most tedious to come down off this wall just to chat about the spiritual weather. We are not bored; we are tired. But it's a good kind of tired.

God thought of us *before our parents did*. Like our elder Brother, we came out of the bosom of the Father and we live and breathe for one reason—to bear witness to the truth throughout the earth.

Like Joseph, we have experienced *three strippings* with our *three anointings*.

In our earlier days, we told the Father's dream to half-brothers, but they sold us out, threw us into a pit, and then lied about it. Later, when we refused to be intimate with the harlot systems of Egypt, we were put in prison by our Father's foreordained design. We have stayed sweet all these years, keeping the living Word in our mouths—a word that means life for some and death for others.

We are now being anointed to go through our third stripping. The first two were easy; somebody else did it for us. But this third unveiling models the *kenosis* or "emptying" of Jesus Christ described in Philippians 2:5-11. The Pattern Son made Himself of no reputation, stripped Himself, and became obedient to the death of the cross. Likewise, our prison garments are coming off. We have shaved, removing the veil from our faces. We are about to come out of prison to reign.

As with Joseph, *our lives have been marked by sovereign confinement.* In the pit, we could but rule our own hearts. In Potiphar's house, we ruled over other people's "stuff." In the prison house, we began to have authority in the hearts of men. *But in the King's court*, we will be given a *measure of rulership over the nations!*[7]

Such is the man or woman who is a mover and shaker in the heavenly corporation. Be strengthened out of Zion in the name of the Lord. You have made a difference. You have walked through fire. Your tears are in His bottle of remembrance. Your prayers have been made a memorial. Now you are about to become the head and not the tail.[8] You will live to see Zion's captivity turned.

Through the years, we have seen all kinds of folks come and go. When the price for corporate anointing dawned on them, they ran. They knew that real commitment and involvement in Body life and ministry were huge responsibilities. *It is expensive to eat from that kind of table.* Count the cost. It will cost you your time, your talent, and your treasure. When you have been called to finish the Father's work, your faith will surely be tested.

Finishing the Father's Work

My theme is the corporate anointing, and it was inspired and fueled by Jesus' prayers that we would become unified into one, even as He and the Father are one.

Jn. 4:34, KJV

> *Jesus saith unto them, My meat is to **do the will of Him that sent Me**, and to **finish His work**.*

Jesus' food and drink, His very sustenance, was to do the "will" of the Father. The Greek word for "will" is *thelema*, and means "a determination, choice, purpose, decree." Its root *thelo* means "desire, delight."[9] Whatever pleased the Father pleased the Pattern Son.[10] Jesus' ministerial goal was to "finish," to "complete, accomplish, consummate" His Father's "work" (or His "acts and deeds"). The Father's work was summed up by the apostle Paul:

2 Cor. 5:18-20, KJV

> *And all things are of God, who hath reconciled us to Himself by Jesus Christ, and hath given to us the ministry of reconciliation;*
>
> *To wit, that **God was in Christ, reconciling the world unto Himself**....*

Now then we are ambassadors for Christ....

Eph. 1:9-10, KJV

Having made known unto us the mystery of His will, according to His good pleasure which He hath purposed in Himself:

*That in the dispensation of the fulness of times He might **gather together in one all things in Christ**, both which are in heaven, and which are on earth; even in Him.*

We are "ambassadors" and the Church is an embassy. This word in Second Corinthians 5:20 in the Greek is *presbeuo*, and is akin to *presbuteros*, the Greek word for "elder."[11] It takes a mature man or woman to participate in the ministry of reconciliation.[12] Yet in Christ, we can stand between two warring spirits and swallow up the death and hell in both without becoming contaminated! The sacred secret of the Father's delight and design that He has "purposed" or "set before" Himself is to "gather together," to "sum up, head up" all things in Heaven and on earth in Christ.

Corporate anointing and unity on its grandest scale transcends time and space.

There is a great drawing, a great gathering going on right now. Jesus adds and multiplies; the devil subtracts and divides. Anything that *separates us* is an enemy to the Father's purpose. Let me say that again: *Anything that separates us is an enemy to the Father's purpose.* We are vessels created to carry anointing. Either *Jesus* will anoint us to *mobilize* or *satan* will anoint us to *scatter*.[13]

The Lord Jesus fearlessly and aggressively did the work of the Father in chapter 4 of John's Gospel, when He risked much to talk to a Samaritan woman. Two of the most powerful deterrents to the Father's will are prejudice with regard to gender and race.[14]

Jn. 4:9, KJV

*Then saith the woman of Samaria unto Him, How is it that Thou, being a Jew, askest drink of me, which am a woman of Samaria? for **the Jews have no dealings with the Samaritans**.*

Jn. 4:27, KJV

*And upon this came His disciples, and **marvelled that He talked with the woman**....*

The Greek word for "dealings" in John 4:9 means "to use jointly; to have intercourse in common." It is taken from two Greek words: *sun* ("with") and *chraomai* ("to use").[15] The New International Version says that "Jews do not associate with Samaritans."

His disciples "marvelled" or "wondered at" the fact that He even talked with this woman. However, the Master wasn't interested in being politically correct. He disrupted His "seeker-sensitive staff" and boldly bucked a millennium of tradition that day! Somebody said, "Don't rock the boat!" I agree. Let's blow it up!

More than a century ago, our great nation was torn asunder by the Civil War. Today, Confederate flags flying over Southern courthouses still make waves because feelings run deep. Some of us have been called to *finish the Father's work*. There is an apostolic mandate upon us to destroy gender prejudice and racial prejudice in the Body of Christ and the world.

Jesus unashamedly talked with that "fallen" woman from the "wrong race" at the well, and He was bucking racial tension between the Jews and Samaritans that didn't go back a few hundred years—it went back over a thousand

years! That's a long time to hold a grudge. Jews and
Samaritans hated each other on a millennial level![16] The
kingdom had divided *generations earlier* in the days of
Rehoboam and Jeroboam.[17] The Samaritans even had their
own Bible or Pentateuch.

Things were made worse by the fact that this woman had
had five husbands, and was flirting with number six! That's
a picture of the Church married to the five natural senses,
and then cavorting with all that man desires. But when she
met the seventh Man, the perfect Man, she dropped her
waterpot and *became* a waterpot! She lost all her fear of
men and boldly proclaimed Christ. As an evangelist, she
laid the groundwork for Philip's citywide revival in Acts 8!

And Their Works Do Follow Them

Jn. 4:35-38, KJV

*Say not ye, There are yet four months, and then
cometh harvest? behold, I say unto you, Lift up your
eyes, and look on the fields; for they are white
already to harvest.*

*And he that reapeth receiveth wages, and gath-
ereth fruit unto life eternal: that both he that soweth
and he that reapeth may rejoice together.*

*And herein is that saying true, One soweth, and
another reapeth.*

*I sent you to reap that whereon ye bestowed no
labour: other men laboured, and **ye are entered into
their labours**.*

Rev. 14:13, KJV

*...that they may rest from their labours; and **their
works do follow them**.*

The modern Church has "entered into" other men's labors. The Greek word for "labors" in John 4:38 and Revelation 14:13 is *kopos*. It means "a cut, (by analogy) toil (as reducing the strength); pains; as in labor with trouble and weariness."[18]

Many years ago here in my home county, men were preaching the gospel of the Kingdom. I have "entered into their labors." Other saints from previous generations have watered *your ground* with *their intercession*. Their works *do* follow them, and God has not forgotten their work and labor of love.[19] You may be reaping where you did not sow, but God says that part of the plan is for those who sow and those who reap to experience the joy of harvest "together."

Corporate anointing and generational purpose are greater than any one person or local church. Compare them to the efforts of a 440- or 880-yard relay team during a track meet. The best and fastest runner is always saved for the *last leg* when the speed advantage matters the most. When he or she wins, the *whole team* wins! Similarly, God has saved the best wine for last![20]

The team concept of ministry is bigger than your church staff: We need to remember that as we cross the Jordan ourselves, we are also "carrying the bones of Joseph"![21] The patriarch wanted to be buried near the family plot.[22] Like Elisha's bones, those bones still have life in them![23] *Remember, "Christ" never left the planet.* When these men and women of God who went before us died, they left us their anointing plus a whole lot more. Their hopes, dreams, aspirations, and even their frustrations have been handed down to us through the decades and centuries. The Lord who kept their "tears in [His] bottle" is about to pour them out upon our unclean lack of vision and courage (Ps. 56:8).

If you don't understand this *transcendent glory*—if you fail to perceive the countless prayers, supernatural answers to prayers, and the corporate anointing that *went before you* and *will continue on long after you*—you will faint. The accuser will come and whisper, "If you were *really* living for God, all this wouldn't be happening to you."

The corporate Son of God and the corporate son of satan are facing off in the Day of the Lord. All hell is breaking loose against men and women who are finishing *the Father's work of reconciliation.* By God's grace, we will tear down every wall! Yes, there is a powerful struggle! But on the other side of every great struggle there is a great harvest. The Church is in its *third trimester of spiritual pregnancy.* Some of us are "showing," and our condition can't be hidden! Once you hear this living Word in your spirit, it's too late.

They Without Us

The Father is heading up everything in Christ. There is a great gathering in the heavenlies that is about to manifest in the earth. This great pressure of birthing the corporate Christ is coming from an army on *each side of the veil*[24]— those who have *died* in Christ and *we who are alive and remain.*[25] This gathering is taking place from one end of Heaven to the other.[26]

Gen. 49:10, KJV

>   ...*unto Him shall the gathering of the people be.*

We are being *gathered into one* by the *voice of One.*[27] This assemblage is not taking place in the realm of the body (natural things) or of the soul; it is taking place in the realm of spirit. It is not a gathering unto black or white, male or female, Jew or Greek. It is not a gathering unto a building, a choir, a preacher, or a message. Neither is it a gathering unto an experience, or unto knowledge. This gathering is unto *Him*!

You must see something bigger than yourself. Some preachers are worried about other preachers using "their stuff," their messages. I just tell them, "Begin to praise God. That's a compliment. If it came from Heaven, then it's not yours. If it didn't, then you don't want it! Go read John 3:27 again and get over it."[28]

Most men are enamored with themselves and with their own feelings and desires. But God is dealing with our souls to *bring forth Christ*. Men still endeavor to establish their identity in something *outside* of Christ, but that which is born of the Spirit is essentially spirit.[29] A Christian is a spirit being of which God Almighty is the Father.[30] Our problem is that we still see *flesh* instead of spirit.[31]

The corporate anointing transcends time and space. It surpasses denominational and sectarian spirits. The only reason we have a "Baptist Jesus," a "Methodist Jesus," a "Pentecostal Jesus," a "Kingdom Jesus" (each with its own emphasis), ad nauseum, is because all of us (and them) have sinned and *come short of the total glory* that He is. He is one with the Father in Heaven, but we have elected to live apart on earth in perpetual divorce while sharing His name and spreading the blame!

Don't create your own external, impersonal God who is comfortable with your sin, one whom you can manipulate and adapt to your own image. We are to be *conformed* to the image of the firstborn Son, and Jesus is the Sum of all the parts. Remember, He is altogether lovely.[32]

Heb. 11:39–12:1, KJV

And these all, having obtained a good report through faith, received not the promise:

*God having provided some better thing for us, that **they without us should not be made perfect**.*

Wherefore seeing we also are compassed about with so great a cloud of witnesses....

The Greek word for "compassed about" here is *perikeimai* and means "to lie all around, inclose, encircle."[33] We learned in the first chapter that *every anointed man or woman who ever died and went to Heaven left his or her mantle with the rest of us!* Their corporate anointing never left the planet. Previous generations have prayed us into the Kingdom, touching our lives. The baton has passed from them to His end-time glorious Church, one holy nation.

Those in the invisible amphitheater of the Book of Hebrews are like midwives, cheering us on to the goal. Why do I say that? Because *we are birthing something unprecedented* in the history of the Church: the *corporate anointing*. This end-time baby is called "Christ." We are carrying the prophetic "burden" of the Lord.[34]

God is so big that He doesn't work through one gender, person, race, or even generation. From the days of Martin Luther (1517) until the Latter Rain revival (1948–1956), the emphasis was upon *the individual*. Then God began shifting gears. His burden now is for *the Body of Christ*, the *corporate Man*.

The birthpangs of the ages are upon us. We have entered into other men's labors, and their works do follow them. They being dead yet speak. They without us shall not be made complete, but praise God, *they do have us!* Jesus said, "The harvest truly is plenteous, but the labourers are few" (Mt. 9:37).[35]

Get this Word of the Kingdom, this incorruptible seed, planted in you and then let it grow till it hurts. Be in labor.

Don't whine. If you do, you will faint. Those who labor, and those who *are in labor*, are few.

So you say you are pregnant. The purpose of God has begun its inevitable march toward full-term delivery in your heart. Now what do you do? Now it is time for us to consider the practical dynamics of and our proper responses to this glorious *corporate anointing* of God.

Chapter Twelve

Our Responsibility to the Corporate Anointing

"...it is required...."

1 Corinthians 4:2

We've come to the final chapter of this book and to a new chapter in our lives. We need to account for all the things that the Holy Spirit has deposited in our hearts and minds at this point before we go onward and upward even more.

We've learned and confirmed that *the anointing is a Person*, the "Spirit of the Son" sent by the Father, and we realize that He is three-dimensional as well. His anointing is *poured out* in Passover, *smeared on* in Pentecost, and *rubbed in* during the Feast of Tabernacles.

Although both Testaments of the Bible explore the *compound anointing*, the foundational model of this holy anointing is the art of the Levitical apothecary established by God in the days of Moses. Pure myrrh, sweet cinnamon, sweet calamus, and cassia were mingled with olive oil to anoint the *whole house*.

The "church in the wilderness" (the children of Israel in the Sinai wilderness) prefigured the end-time Body of Christ. Under the headship of Moses, they were *kept*, *delivered*, *supplied*, *instructed*, and *sifted*.

We discovered that the *compound anointing oil* also reveals the glorious unity of the Spirit and the many aspects of the *compound names of God*.

The truth concerning corporate anointing is vast; it is generational, transcending time and space. There remains but one question: What is our *individual* and *collective* responsibility to this corporate anointing?

Four Gates to Your World

Lk. 12:48, KJV

*...For unto whomsoever much is given, of him shall be much **required**....*

1 Cor. 4:2, KJV

*Moreover it is **required** in stewards, that a man be found faithful.*

The word for "required" in these verses means "to seek after; to require, demand."[1] It implies a search for something hidden. The Living Bible says that "...their responsibility is greater."

The purpose of every enemy of Israel in the Old Testament was *to keep the Israelites from becoming a nation*, a people unto God. The devil, the ultimate enemy of mankind and of God's purposes for us, made every attempt to *abort the Messianic seed*, and to destroy or contaminate the Israelites' corporate effectiveness. This same demonic attitude was especially apparent in the actions of the Edomites, who were direct descendants of Esau. They clearly represent the flesh.

The enemy will do everything to frustrate *your* understanding and pursuit of corporate anointing as well—but that doesn't mean you should helplessly stand aside while his efforts succeed. Let me put arrows in your bow, stones in your sling, and bullets in your gun. Let me show you practical (and thoroughly biblical) ways to be salt and light in the earth and confound your enemy.

There are *four gates* to the world you live in and work in every day:

1. Your **home and family**.

2. Your **local church**.

3. Your **job**.

4. Your **community**.

To be a "joint of supply" in any of these four areas means that you must be *covenantally joined*.[2] In other words, it takes at least two. You cannot be a joint by yourself. A joint must be joined. With regard to any level of human relationships, "What therefore God hath joined together, let not man put asunder" (Mt. 19:6b). Jesus Himself personally promised that wherever *two are joined together* in His name, He would come and be the "third" party to join in the union of heart and soul.[3]

Your Home and Family

Responsibility to corporate anointing begins at home. Every local church problem is a home problem. The main issue is that we have stopped doing things *together*. The solution is deceptively simple: Turn off all the other distractions and talk to each other. Eat meals and the right kinds of foods together. If you are too busy, simplify your lifestyle.

Marriage itself is "an apothecary thing." Two have become one. God mingles two people together to form a brand-new entity in every marriage, so marriage is *more than a partnership*. It is a merger of identities. For that reason, no one will "make you" or "break you" like your mate.

Serve the Lord by serving your husband or your wife. Submission to authority in the fear of the Lord goes both ways.[4] Let there be mutual respect and honor given at all times. *Never* argue in front of your children, and *never* let the sun go down on your wrath.[5]

If you are a "young person" and are still living with your parents, then you need to realize that *your room* is your part of the Kingdom of God. Your necessary part is to keep it clean. Never talk back to your parents, especially your mother. That's rebellion, witches' brew. Take care of the basics. For instance, do your homework before you watch television. Do your own laundry. Learn how to cook. Do the dishes without being asked.

Is this too spiritual for you?

My "prophetic word" to children of all ages is equally simple: Tithe on your allowance. Do what your parents ask you to do when they ask you do it. And do it with a right spirit, which is the joy of the Lord.

Can you imagine a home where no one person feels weak, or insecure, or insignificant?

I ask you—whether you are a husband, a wife, a parent, or a child—have you ever considered the fact that God wants to make your family name great? According to the apostle Paul, Christians are Abraham's seed by the Spirit,[6] and God's promise to this powerful man of faith was direct and to the point:

Gen. 12:2, KJV

*And I will make of thee a great nation, and I will bless thee, and **make thy name great**....*

The Hebrew word for "great" means "to become strong, grow up, be great or wealthy, evidence oneself as being great (magnified), be powerful, significant, or valuable."[7] This word is prophesying to you and your family.

I was an only child, and my dad died when I was 17. Only recently have I begun to understand the generational purposes of God that we discussed in the previous chapter. And for whatever reasons, I have only recently contemplated the truth that *God wants,* by His grace and mercy, *to take the name of "Varner" and make it great in the earth.* I am eager for you to discover this same treasure from Heaven for your family and your name.

God honors His man and His woman, and so He will honor the name of every family that faithfully serves Him.

Your Local Church

The local church is a spiritual family compounded by the great Apothecary from many natural families. *Every Christian needs a local church and a godly pastor.* No one is exempt from this truth. No one. And once God places us in His body,[8] then we each need to be faithful to invest that body with our time, talent, and tithe.

Many churches are entertainment-based, need-oriented, and man-centered. That emphasis must change—from "I, me, and mine" unto "we" and "us."

If you are a pastor, then I am under obligation of the Spirit to tell you that *you will never be a success without a successor.* Broaden your leadership base. Learn how to delegate authority and give away lesser responsibilities. Share your pulpit. May I suggest that every time your local body of believers meets, that you set aside some time for one of your leaders (be they elders, deacons, or fivefold ministers "in training") to minister the Word of God before *you* do. Rotate through your roster of leaders and train them in the work of the ministry.

Why am I saying this? It is the job of the "set man or woman" (the individual "set" into senior leadership by God), the watchman, to watch the anointing on the people. Sheep reproduce sheep, but shepherds are to *reproduce shepherds.* Equip them and then *put them to work*!

I know some won't like what I'm saying, because many preachers want to be the center of attention. This tendency isn't helped by the fact that a lot of people want a preacher and not a pastor. They want the blessing without the procedure. They don't want to hear about such things as *covenantal commitment* and *corporate responsibility.*

Most of the people in the Evangelical and Pentecostal/Charismatic church world have been used to "voting out" any preacher they didn't like. Then they would just "vote in" one who would do as they asked. Real Kingdom order is theocratic (or *God-ruled* through His delegated authority), not democratic. The central focus under God's government is that leaders—and believers in all positions—do what *He* asks! (And God *never* takes popularity polls.) The only final authorities consulted by God's "set" leaders in times of difficulty or decision are God's Word and God's Spirit.

Everyone in the local church should be trained about corporate anointing. Did you realize that your hearty "amen" and positive response during good preaching is the

Apothecary at work? When folks first get saved, tell them, "Welcome to the Kingdom of God. We're glad to have you. Now you need to know that you cannot have God without having His people. We're in this and *in Him* together."

There are different burdens for different aspects of every local work. We desperately need to learn to respect and honor our differences. As members of a corporate body, we need to stop thinking less of each other simply because *we don't love to do the same things*. We are all called to speak the same thing,[9] but we don't speak the same thing the same way. There are different operations of "energies" or anointings.[10]

God wants the *horizontal release* of that which has been *vertically realized* and "set."[11] We're about to realize a "saints" movement. Everything we receive from God should show up in our everyday relationships with one another! We can only minister life to others from what and who we are in Christ. What are you good at? What things do you love to do? Don't be shocked when I say that God gave you those abilities and loves. Everyone wants to "know God's will" for their lives, but I say that they need to begin with the answers to these simple questions: a) "What do you *want* to do?" and b) "When do you want to start?"

Your Job

Your work environment or vocation offers one of the ripest of all opportunities for the *corporate anointing* to work through your life. To begin with, God wants to use *you* to "leaven the whole lump." Begin the day by praying for your employer and your fellow employees. *There's enough of God in you to impact the whole place*—if you release it. When you pray, prophesy and decree some things into being and God will establish them.[12]

On the practical side, make sure that you are an *asset* and not a liability or loss to your employer or clients. You represent Christ Jesus Himself, so do your job right the first time. Give 150 percent, not just 100 percent. Work for the company as though you owned it. Who knows? One day you might. If you work for clients, then work for them as you would work for yourself!

Refuse to listen to gossip at the water cooler or anyplace else. If all else fails, tell the mouthy people who persist in smearing their gossip on you, "Would you please write that down and sign it?" If the person doesn't take the hint, be bolder, "My ears aren't slop buckets!" If that won't help the talebearer, pray him out the door. Be jealous for your boss and those who work with you. Refuse to hear an evil report in the absence of the person being discussed. Be flexible and merciful with regard to work schedules.

If you want a raise, begin to tithe on the amount you want to get. Let God be your source. Why do you want more money? To buy more non-essentials, or to bless the Kingdom of God, especially missionaries in other nations?

Let God promote you.[13] If you compete in the flesh, God will let you stew in your own juices. Remember, you can mingle the right ingredients and make *anointing oil*, or you can mix the wrong stuff together and make a witches' brew that may become embalming fluid *for you*![14]

Your Community

Christians, pastors, and local churches have a glorious opportunity to impact their entire community. Let me ask you a supposedly hypothetical question: "What would happen in any given locale if there were no religious competition among God's people?" I say "supposedly" because the competition has never been God's idea or doing. Remember

Jesus' high priestly prayer that we be one as He and the Father are one? Jesus said our unity and love one for another would be our only outward distinguishing mark to the world! Preachers *must* pray together. Churches *must* serve together. I don't care what you do—just do it *together*! The fact that we *are together* is just as important as what we are attempting to do.

Get to know and pray for your city fathers and civil leaders. Bless the police department, the fire department, and the rescue squad. When our church did this, we not only fed these local leaders and public safety personnel, but we also gave them plaques of appreciation. Our church leadership told them the truth, that "they were doing the work of the Kingdom" in our little town. We reminded them that Jesus taught, "Greater love hath no man than this, that a man lay down his life for his friends" (Jn. 15:13). When these brave men and women answer a domestic disturbance or prowler call, they have no guarantee of the outcome (because people are crazy). In this day, our public servants put their lives in danger constantly. That is why we need to *show them corporate anointing*.

Let your life and the ministry of your local church make a real difference in your community. Open yourself up to others.

Face to Face

There was one piece of furniture in the Most Holy Place, the realm of anointed glory: the Ark of the Covenant and its golden lid called "the mercy seat." Made of one piece of gold, the mercy seat was united with two cherubim—facing each other.

In a grander sense, these heavenly beings picture the Old Testament and the New Testament saints fronting each other, both focused on the blood in between.[15] Our spiritual ancestors looked ahead to the cross and, like Moses, saw God's hind parts, the back side of the cross.[16] We, on the other hand, look back to the same cross as a *finished work*, beholding the face of Jesus Christ.[17] A similar scene lies before us in chapter 6 of Isaiah.

Is. 6:3, KJV

> *And one cried unto another, and said, Holy, holy, holy, is the Lord of hosts: the whole earth is full of His glory.*

Isaiah the prophet had been declaring "woe" unto everything until he saw the throne room and heard another voice—the sound of resurrection life coming from within the veil, from between the wings of the seraphim.

Calvary predicated Pentecost. First came the blood, then the oil. Jesus' blood makes corporate anointing possible. When we are focused on the blood, we can face each other—in the home or church, on the job, or anywhere in town. Because we are looking at each other through the blood, we can boldly prophesy to each other, *"Holy, holy, holy!"* in unison with the four cherubim, the angelic hosts, and the "four and twenty elders" of John's revelation (Rev. 4:8-10). Those who catch this vision of corporate anointing will discover that they can say and sing little else until "the whole earth is full of His glory"!

Some Assembly Required

Heb. 10:25-26, KJV

> *Not forsaking **the assembling of ourselves together**, as the manner of some is; but exhorting one another: and so much the more, as ye see the day approaching.*

For if we sin wilfully after that we have received the knowledge of the truth, there remaineth no more sacrifice for sins.

We are like a bicycle in a box. All the parts are there, but they have to be put together. The Manufacturer warns us: "Some Assembly Required." Thank God for the Bible, the instruction manual.

All the ingredients for the apothecary were contained in the garden of the Shulamite.[18] They need only be assembled. The word for "assembling" in Hebrews 10:25 is *episunagoge*, which means "a complete collection; especially a Christian meeting (for worship)." It means "to collect upon the same place" and is also translated as "gathering together" in the King James Version.[19]

Too many times *we gather without assembling*. We managed to seat all our bodies together in the same building, but our minds and spirits are someplace else! We need to be *compacted together*.[20]

If we sin willfully after we have received the "knowledge" of the truth about corporate anointing, it's serious (Heb. 10:26). This word means "recognition, full discernment, acknowledgment."[21] There remains no more sacrifice for sin, because there is not another sacrifice. Jesus is the only One who can put us together as He alone builds His Church.

What Is in Your House?

2 Kings 4:2, KJV

*And Elisha said unto her, What shall I do for thee? tell me, **what hast thou in the house?** And she said, Thine handmaid hath not any thing in the house, **save a pot of oil**.*

This woman is a picture of the Church. She has all the spices in her pot, but doesn't know what to do with them. The prophet instructed her to bring vessels, and "not a few" either (2 Kings 4:3-7). These imported vessels can represent mobile, translocal ministries. But the basic answer to her problem and the cure for her debt *was in her own pot.*

To every individual and pastor I ask, "What is in your house?"

We always want to be like someone else. Tall people slump over. Short people wear elevator shoes. Thin folks want to gain weight and heavy folks want to be thin. Some blacks want to be white, and whites lay out in the sun all day to make themselves black. Look in the mirror. You are fearfully and wonderfully made.[22] Be bold. Ask the Father to show you *the ingredients of your own pot.* You are very special, an original design.

Pastor, why are you going all over the country to find the mind of God for your city? We cut and paste, frantically searching for the right pattern. We bring home "a nose" from a local body here and "an arm" from a local body over there, only to build a Frankenstein's monster at home. There's no life in trying to build somebody else's vision using somebody else's parts! That's a false mixture without any anointing.

Our churches and Bible conventions are filled with people who haven't prayed, who instead rush back and forth from one to another asking, "What's hot? What's not?" I declare to them in the name of the Lord:

"Stop cloning the sheep and get your *own* revival! Everything you need to stop the deficit is already in your own house![23] Assess the need of *your* city. Get before God and find out what He wants *you* to do."

Excuses

The truth is that behind every excuse there is a lack of desire. Sometimes it seems the only way Christian folks move into "one mind" is when they come up with the *same old excuses*!

Lk. 14:16-20, KJV

> *Then said He unto him, A certain man made a great supper, and bade many:*
>
> *And sent his servant at supper time to say to them that were bidden, Come; for all things are now ready.*
>
> *And they all with one consent began to make excuse. The first said unto him, I have bought a piece of ground, and I must needs go and see it: I pray thee have me excused.*
>
> *And another said, I have bought five yoke of oxen, and I go to prove them: I pray thee have me excused.*
>
> *And another said, I have married a wife, and therefore I cannot come.*

The great supper is the *world harvest* of the Feast of Tabernacles, the feast of unity and glory. The sent servant is the Holy Ghost. Everything is ready, adjusted, and prepared, because corporate anointing is based upon the *finished* work of Jesus.

Sadly, too many are like Judas, who couldn't wait three more hours for the perfect hanging (Jesus' crucifixion), so he went out and hanged himself. The weakness of his own reasonings caused the son of perdition to fall headlong; he couldn't wait.[24] Abraham took matters into his own hands and gave birth to a wild man who "looked" like the son of promise but became the father of his adversaries. The problem was that Ishmael had a foreign heart like his momma!

Jesus said problems began when everyone in His parable began to move in the wrong kind of unity—with *"one consent"* they began to *"make excuse"* (Lk. 14:18). The Greek word translated as "excuse" is *paraiteomai*, and it means "to beg off, deprecate, decline, shun." It is also translated as "to avoid, refuse, reject" in the King James Version.[25] It comes from two words: *para* ("aside") and *aiteo* ("to ask"). Those who make excuses like to whisper in corners. They will stand alongside, but won't get close enough to be involved with corporate anointing.

"I Would Rather Count My Possessions"

This first excuse describes far too many American Christians. They bought the bill of goods before they saw it for what it was. They have been hoodwinked and bamboozled by money-grabbing spiritual peddlers who have corrupted the Word of God.[26] Both the peddlers and the duped need to read the Bible. A man who does not read cannot think. What you will be five years from now will be the result of the books you are reading today, and the people with whom you are relating in intimate relationships.

"I Prefer to Do Something Else (More Important to Me)"

The second excuse deals with preachers and believers who have entrenched themselves in their comfort zones. Many of these are proven ministries in the Pentecostal realm and the fivefold ministry gifts, but they refuse to go on to know Him *in His Lordship*. Preachers who are in this thing for the money know that if you keep the people in a state of constant need, they will keep coming back to be "delivered" over and over again...and the pay is good. People will let you pour oil (the candlestick), bake bread (the table), and make incense (golden altar) until you drop. I know how to move in the gifts of the Spirit, I can exegete the Scriptures, and I am a prophetic psalmist. They all have their place, but *I'd rather teach the corporate Man how to do them!*[27]

"I Am Married to Something (or Someone) More Important Than God"

The third excuse describes those who have married a spouse, a job, a family, or a religious organization. By clinging to this claim, we are declaring that we prefer to nestle between the withered breasts of harlot systems (prostituting our gifts and callings outside of the covenant) than to draw from the nourishment of El-Shaddai! God forbid!

Not understanding the King or His Kingdom, folks in the American Church still think that they have choices. In truth there is "Plan A" and there is "Plan A"! (That's right— there is *no* "Plan B.")

> "Jonah, you are going to Nineveh. You will learn to overcome your prejudice and participate in compound anointing. In the first 'Plan A' God will pay your way. The other 'Plan A' is for you to pay the fare (Jon. 1:3). Either way, you are going to Nineveh— there's a connecting flight."

You can tell if a man is running from the Word of the Lord—he's like Jonah, creating a storm for everybody else! Don't mar His visage and corporate anointing by pandering to your own insecurities and individualism.[28] If you haven't realized it yet, you should know that *God is trying to kill you* and *the devil is trying to kill you* too! One death leads to true life; the other death leads to true death.

You are going to die no matter what you do, so be like the old prophet Simeon. His aged feet were planted in *one age* while in his arms he beheld *the age to come*—the Christ, Jesus the Messiah. This wise man had been told that he would not see death until he had seen "the Lord's Christ" (Lk. 2:26). When you see and understand the *collective anointing of the corporate Christ* that spans the ages, *you will die the right kind of death* as old Simeon did.

Ye Have Not Passed This Way Heretofore

Everything in the earth is accelerating. It took 400 years to get through the Outer Court (1517–1906) and only 50 years to get through the Holy Place.

Jesus is coming!

But until we change, Jesus cannot return to this planet. Jesus is coming back, but He cannot come until:

1. His enemies are made His footstool in the earth.[29] Racism and every other kind of prejudice is an enemy to unity and glory.

2. The time of the restoration of all things of which the prophets have spoken.[30] It is during this time that God will restore the years.[31]

3. The Church comes into the unity of the faith (corporate anointing), the full and accurate knowledge of the Son of God, and attains to the measure of the full stature of Christ.[32] This can only happen through the apothecary function of the fivefold ministries as they press and compact the saints for the work of the ministry in the power of unity. This is the heart of the corporate anointing.

4. The heavenly Husbandman receives the early and latter rains.[33] Both will be poured out in the "first," a firstfruits corporate company unto God and the Lamb.[34] This message of reconciliation is one of the hardest to proclaim. People like preaching that fights against the devil or some organization

because messages that are "against something" are usually fiery and exciting. To every preacher, I direct a simple question: "What are you for?" Folks do not like to hear words of correction that call for personal and corporate repentance in attitudes and works. People do not like change, yet the very process of glorification involves being "changed into the same image from glory to glory" (2 Cor. 3:18).

Josh. 3:3-4, KJV

And they commanded the people, saying, When ye see the ark of the covenant of the Lord your God, and the priests the Levites bearing it, then ye shall remove from your place, and go after it.

Yet there shall be a space between you and it, about two thousand cubits by measure: come not near unto it, that ye may know the way by which ye must go: for ye ***have not passed this way heretofore****.*

The Church has been brought out of Egypt and led through the wilderness. Moses the shepherd has passed the baton to Joshua the soldier. A third baptism is before us. The river is flooded in the days of world harvest.

There is a *corporate Man* with a multifaceted anointing that has begun to stir himself. The spices have begun to cook and blend. When you see priests who have been sanctified by blood and oil take hold of the *same burden* and uphold the Ark of God, the Lordship of Jesus, then you know it's time to arise and move.

Remove from your place, and go after it.

Remove from out of your past, your unbelief, your procrastination, your envy and jealousy, your bitterness, your worry, your excuses, and your feelings of insufficiency...

Get up and move out of your individualism.

Bring your spice and mingle it.

On an old rugged cross just outside the city of Jerusalem, Jesus of Nazareth rent the veil, just as the Ark split the Jordan River in Joshua's day.

In Joshua 3:16, we are told the waters of the Jordan backed up all the way to "*the city Adam*, that is beside *Zaretan*" [meaning "to pierce or puncture"[35]].

The finished work of our Savior, whose side is pierced, cut off every hindering flow *all the way back to Adam*! Now, 2,000 cubits—and 2,000 years—later, a holy nation, a corporate Man with a kingly crown upon His Head and the robes of royalty about His many-membered Body, has compounded the anointing after the art of the apothecary. Now He has risen in all of His glory, and is about to possess the land of promise!

You are a principal spice, a necessary part, a vital ingredient to this present move of God in the earth.

General Joshua, *Yehosua* the Captain of our salvation, is speaking to you if you have ears to hear:

"*Sanctify yourselves: for to morrow the Lord will do wonders among you*" (Josh. 3:5b)!

Endnotes

Introduction

1. *Webster's New Universal Unabridged Dictionary* (Cleveland, OH: Dorset & Baber, n.d.).

2. This urgency isn't new to me. The last line of my book, *The Three Prejudices* (Shippensburg, PA: Destiny Image, 1997), declared, "We have yet to sing the kind of song we are capable of singing—together." The keynote of another writing, *The Time of the Messiah* (Shippensburg, PA: Destiny Image, 1996), was the revelation of the corporate Messiah, the end-time Body of Christ—one holy, "enchristed seed."

Chapter One

1. Eph. 1:10.

2. Ex. 40:13-15; 1 Sam. 16:1,13; 1 Kings 19:16.

3. Acts 3:22-23; Heb. 7:26; Rev. 19:16.

4. 1 Pet. 2:9; Rev. 1:6; 5:10.

5. God the Holy Spirit is clearly named and honored in Jn. 14:16-17,26; 15:26; 16:7-8,13-15.

6. Jn. 14:2,23.

7. 1 Cor. 3:16-17; 6:19; 2 Cor. 6:16; Eph. 2:19-22.

8. 1 Cor. 11:29.

9. 1 Cor. 12:8-10; Eph. 4:11.

10. 2 Pet. 3:8.

11. Col. 2:19.

12. 1 Cor. 6:17.

13. 2 Cor. 4:4.

14. Rom. 8:29; compare Gen. 1:26-28; Ps. 22:22; Is. 8:18; Heb. 2:6-13.

15. Num. 11:24-25; 1 Tim. 2:5.

16. Gal. 4:19.

17. Heb. 12:22-23.

18. Strong's, #H117.

19. Rom. 8:17.

20. 2 Kings 2:13.

21. Mal. 4:5-6; Mt. 17:10-13.

22. Acts 8:16; 10:44; 11:15.

23. Strong's, #G1968.

24. Rom. 5:5.

25. Heb. 11:39–12:2.

26. Ezek 47:1-5; compare Jn. 7:37-39.

27. Hos. 6:1-3.

28. Ex. 7:8-13.

29. 1 Kings 18:21-40.

30. Acts 8:9-24; 13:6-11.

31. Jn. 12:24.

32. Acts 2:33-36.

33. 2 Kings 4:1-7.

34. Rev. 1:12-15.

Chapter Two

1. Deut. 19:15; Mt. 18:16; 2 Cor. 13:1.

2. Strong's, #H7991, H7969.

3. Ps. 84:7; Rom. 1:17; 2 Cor. 3:18.

4. Deut. 16:16.

5. This threefold principle is discussed in depth in the first chapters of each of my following three volumes known as "the trilogy": *Prevail—A Handbook for the Overcomer* (see pages 84-85 for 40 examples of threefold things [Shippensburg, PA: Destiny Image, 1982]); *The*

More Excellent Ministry (Shippensburg, PA: Destiny Image, 1988); and *The Priesthood Is Changing* (Shippensburg, PA: Destiny Image, 1991).

6. Strong's, #H5480.

7. R. Laird Harris, Gleason L. Archer, Jr., Bruce K. Waltke, eds., *The Theological Wordbook of the Old Testament*, Vol. II (Chicago, IL: Moody Press, 1980), 619. (Author's note: *Sûk* also occurs in Deut. 28:40; 2 Sam. 14:2; Dan. 10:3; Mic. 6:15.)

8. Rom. 8:11.

9. Strong's, #H4886.

10. R. Laird Harris, Gleason L. Archer, Jr., Bruce K. Waltke, eds., *The Theological Wordbook of the Old Testament*, Vol. I (Chicago, IL: Moody Press, 1980), 530-531.

11. Ex. 29:7; 30:30; Num. 35:25.

12. 2 Sam. 12:7; compare 1 Kings 19:15-16.

13. Is. 61:1; Dan. 9:24.

14. Strong's, #H4899.

15. 1 Sam. 2:10; 2 Sam. 22:51; Ps. 2:2; 18:50; compare Dan. 9:25-26.

16. Strong's, #G218.

17. Strong's, #G5548.

18. Lk. 4:18; Acts 4:27; 10:38; Heb. 1:9.

19. 2 Cor. 1:21.

20. Ex. 28:41; 1 Sam. 10:1; 1 Kings 19:16.

21. Strong's, #G5545.

22. Jn. 3:34.

23. Also Rev. 1:4; 4:5; 5:6.

24. Mt. 13:21.

25. 2 Cor. 2:16.

26. Eph. 3:17-19.

27. 1 Sam. 9:2; 10:23.

28. Heb. 1:9.

29. Lk. 4:1-14; 1 Jn. 2:15-17.

30. Jn. 16:13.

31. Is. 61:3.

32. Rev. 1:6; 5:10.

33. 2 Pet. 1:5.

34. Is. 40:2; Jn. 19:30.

35. 1 Jn. 2:20,27.

36. 1 Cor. 6:17.

37. Mt. 7:14; Phil. 3:12-14.

38. Gen. 1:26-28.

39. Acts 10:38.

40. Lk. 1:35; 3:21-22.

41. Rom. 8:14.

42. Rev. 5:6.

Chapter Three

1. Gen. 1:4,10,12,18,21,25.

2. 2 Cor. 5:17; Rev. 4:11.

3. When God said "every thing" He had made was "very good" in Genesis 1:31, the Hebrew adverb translated as "very" is *me'od*. It means "vehemently, wholly, speedily (often with other words as an intensive or superlative)." It can also mean "exceedingly, greatly, highly" (Strong's, #H3966).

4. This is in stark contrast to the "vanity of vanities" of the Book of Ecclesiastes (Eccles. 1:2).

5. Interpreted from Strong's #H3605 and #H3634, respectively.

6. Heb. 8:1.

7. Num. 14:21.

8. By "third-day people" I refer to people who live and serve in the third and highest realm of revelation, intimacy, and union with Jesus Christ. This is one of the most powerful illustrations of the dynamic of threes in God's Word, and can be best understood by thoroughly understanding the "threes" of the Tabernacle of Moses—consisting of the Outer Court, the Holy Place, and the Most Holy Place. We will deal with this in more detail in later chapters.

9. Gen. 1:26-28; 2 Cor. 3:18.

10. Strong's, #G3954. Author's note: This word is also translated as "confidence" in the King James Version (see Acts 28:31; Heb. 3:6; 10:35; 1 Jn. 2:28; 3:21; 5:14).

11. Dan. 2:47; Rev. 17:14; 19:16.

12. Similarly, there was one "cloud" before Jesus' death, burial, resurrection, and ascension. After that, the Bible mentions "clouds" (Mt. 26:64; 1 Thess. 4:17; Rev. 1:7).

13. "Servants" also appears in Isaiah 56:6; 63:17; 65:8-9,13-15; 66:14.

14. The material for this section is taken from my book *Understanding Types, Shadows, and Names*, Vol. 1 (Shippensburg, PA: Destiny Image, 1996).

15. See also Lev. 21:20; Acts 2:42-47; Eph. 3:10,15; 1 Pet. 4:10.

16. Strong's, #H811, H810.

17. Col. 1:19; 2:9.

18. Varner, *Understanding Types, Shadows, and Names*, Vol. 1, 229.

19. Varner, *Understanding Types, Shadows, and Names*, Vol. 1, 229.

20. Jer. 31:12.

Chapter Four

1. Col. 1:27.

2. Ex. 30:22-33.

3. Strong's, #H7218.

4. Eph. 1:20-23.

5. Jn. 15:1-5.

6. The plural word for "spices" in Exodus 30:23 means "to be fragrant; an aroma" (Strong's, #H1314).

7. Heb. 4:10.

8. Ps. 120–134; Ezek. 40:26-31.

9. Ex. 25:31-32; Is. 11:1-2. The seven shafts or branches of the Golden Lampstand prefigure the "seven Spirits of God" seen in Revelation 1:4; 3:1; 4:5; 5:6. Its central shaft represents the Spirit of the Lord; then, in poised symmetry, follow the spirit of wisdom and understanding, the spirit of counsel (purpose) and might, and the spirit of knowledge and the fear of the Lord. These branches constitute the fullness of the Spirit, or the Spirit without measure that rested upon the Pattern Son (Jn. 3:34).

10. See Ps. 80:15; Is. 4:2; 60:21; Jer. 23:5; 33:15; Zech. 6:12-13; Jn. 15:1-5.

11. Ps. 68:18; Eph. 4:8-11.

12. Col. 1:27.

13. Strong's, #H4753. Myrrh is twice translated from the Hebrew word *lot*, which means "a gum (from its sticky nature); probably ladanum" (seen only in Gen. 37:25; 43:11—Strong's #H3910). The New Testament Greek word *smurna* is also translated as "myrrh; perfumed oil" (Strong's, #G4666).

14. Strong's, #H4843.

15. Strong's, #H1865.

16. See Lev. 25:10; Is. 61:1; Jer. 34:8,15, twice in 17; and Ezek. 46:17.

17. Jn. 19:39-40; Phil. 3:10.

18. 2 Pet. 1:4-11.

19. Eph. 5:25-27.

20. Prov. 4:20-22.

21. Esther 2:12; 2 Cor. 2:14-16; Eph. 5:1-2.

22. Mt. 2:11.

23. Mk. 15:23.

24. Compare Rom. 8:21; Gal. 2:4; 5:1,13; Jas. 1:25; 2:12.

25. Strong's, #G1657, G1658.

26. Gal. 4:26.

27. 1 Thess. 5:8.

28. Heb. 2:1-11.

29. Much of the material concerning the last three spices of the anointing oil—sweet cinnamon, sweet calamus, and cassia—is taken from Volume 1 of my reference work, *Understanding Types, Shadows, and Names* (Shippensburg, PA: Destiny Image, 1996).

30. Strong's, #H7076.

31. Strong's, #G2792.

32. Strong's, #H1314.

33. Jn. 1:17; 6:27; Acts 10:38.

34. See 2 Sam. 23:1; Dan. 9:24-27; Mt. 1:1; Jn. 1:41; 4:25-26.

35. See also Eph. 5:25-32.

36. Eph. 5:2.

37. Song 2:3.

38. Ps 133; Prov. 27:7; Acts 8:32-33.

39. Song 4:14; Gal. 5:22-23.

40. Ex. 30:32-33; Prov. 7:17; Rev. 18:13.

41. Esther 2:12.

42. Strong's, #H7070.

43. Strong's, #H7069.

44. Gen. 3:15; Acts 2:24.

45. Heb. 1:8.

46. Ezek. 40:3-5; Eph. 4:13.

47. Eph. 5:2; 1 Pet. 1:18-19.

48. Ex. 25:31; Col. 1:18-19; 2:9.

49. Ex. 25:32; Jn. 15:1-7.

50. 1 Cor. 12:8-10; Gal. 5:22-23.

51. Song 4:13-14.

52. 2 Pet. 1:3-4.

53. 2 Cor. 2:15-16.

54. Jn. 15:5.

55. Is. 9:6; Eph. 4:11.

56. 1 Cor. 12:18,28.

57. Jn. 7:37-39.

58. Ezek. 47:1-12.

59. Esther 2:12.

60. Strong's, #H6916.

61. Strong's, #H6915.

62. Phil. 2:5-8.

63. Ex. 29:7; Eph. 1:20-23.

64. See Lev. 8:12; Ps. 45:7; Rom. 8:29; and Lev. 21:10-12; Rev. 19:16, respectively.

65. Rev. 1:6.

66. Ps. 75:6-7; Prov. 15:33.

67. Ex. 29:21; Ps. 133.

68. 1 Cor. 2:16; Phil. 2:5.

69. Gen. 22:5; Rom. 12:1-2.

70. Mk. 14:36; Rom. 8:15; Gal. 4:6.

71. Jn. 14:6; Acts 4:12.

72. Ex. 30:11-16.

73. 1 Cor. 6:20; Gal. 3:13-14.

74. Is. 60:5.

75. Lev. 24:2.

76. Strong's, #G1068.

77. Jn. 19:30.

78. 1 Cor. 12; Rom. 12.

Chapter Five

1. Rom. 8:23; Eph. 1:13-14.

2. Gen. 5:24; Heb. 11:5.

3. Ps. 127:1; Mt. 16:18.

4. Strong's, #H4842. This word, *mirqachath* ("compound"), appears three times in the Old Testament (Ex. 30:25; 1 Chron. 9:30; 2 Chron. 16:14).

5. Strong's, #H7543.

6. Strong's, #H4639.

7. Deut. 11:3,7; Esther 10:2.

8. Strong's, #G1754.

9. See Ex. 30:25,33,35; 37:29; 1 Sam. 8:13; 1 Chron. 9:30; 2 Chron. 16:14; Eccles. 10:1; Ezek. 24:10.

10. Ex. 30:35-36.

11. This is the definition of the term "temper together," from the Hebrew word *malach* (Strong's, #H4414). Compare 1 Cor. 1:10; 14:26; Eph. 2:21-22; 4:16; Col. 2:2,19.

12. Jn. 4:23-24.

13. Lev. 25.

14. Gal. 3:20.

15. Mt. 28:19; Jn. 14:13-17.

16. Jn. 4:24; Heb. 12:29; 1 Jn. 1:5; 4:8.

17. Strong's, #G4856, G4859, as seen in Mt. 18:19.

18. Is. 7:14; 1 Tim. 3:16.

19. Mt. 6:33.

20. 2 Tim. 2:20.

21. Please understand that I am *not* trying to exclude the faithful followers of Christ found in virtually every mainline or historical Christian denomination on earth (including the Roman Catholic Church). What I *am* doing is showing the different levels of intimacy represented by our initial entrance into the Court of His Kingdom (the Outer Court) through salvation in Christ; followed by our entrance through the baptism of the Holy Spirit into the fullness of His gifts for co-laborers together with Him in the Holy Place; and finally our entry into the place of intimacy in the Most Holy Place beyond the veil where all is God. For more information on the deeper life issues of our progression into His presence, you may want to refer to the "trilogy" of books I've written on these topics: *Prevail—A Handbook for the Overcomer*, *The More Excellent Ministry*, and *The Priesthood Is Changing*, all published by Destiny Image Publishers in Shippensburg, Pennsylvania.

22. 1 Jn. 2:12-14.

23. Rom. 10:12.

24. Mt. 13:23.

25. Ps. 72:19; Is. 6:3; Hab. 2:14.

26. Compare Ezek. 43:10-12.

27. Also see Rev. 1:6; 5:10.

28. Eph. 4:11.

29. Mt. 24:37-41.

30. Strong's, #H4971, *mathkoneth* ("composition"); also #H8505.

31. Prov. 7; 31.

32. Rev. 17–19; 21.

33. Heb. 12:25-29.

34. Mt. 7:21-23; 1 Cor. 3:13-15.

35. Col. 1:27.

36. 2 Cor. 6:7.

37. Mt. 12:30.

38. Strong's, #G5331, G5332; see Rev. 9:21; 18:23. Author's note: I realize there are many godly pharmacists who provide a valuable service to mankind today, and I do *not* imply that they are "practicing witchcraft." I am dealing here with strict historical definitions of ancient Greek words used in the anointed writings of the apostles and prophets.

39. Gal. 5:20.

40. 1 Sam. 15:22-23.

41. Strong's, #H2114, *zuwr.*

42. 1 Thess. 5:12; 1 Tim. 5:22; compare Josh. 9:14; Prov. 5:13; 1 Tim. 3:10.

43. 2 Cor. 2:11 and Strong's #G954. The Chaldean word for "fly" is literally *zebuwb*, and one of the Hebrew terms for "lord" is *ba'al* (Strong's, #H2070, H1168).

44. Strong's, #H887, H7381, H7306. Also seen in Gen. 34:30; Ps. 38:5; Prov. 13:5.

45. Ps. 133:2.

46. 2 Pet. 2:15; Jude 11; Rev. 2:14.

47. 2 Kings 4:40.

48. Ex. 30:34.

Chapter Six

1. These books are also known as the Torah and the Law.

2. Strong's, #G4819. The word translated as "happened" is the Greek word *sumbaino*, which means "to walk together."

3. Strong's, #G5179. This same Greek word is rendered as "print" in John 20:25 and "pattern" in Titus 2:7 and Hebrews 8:5.

4. Compare Eph. 6:4; Tit. 3:10.

5. Eph. 1:9-11; 4:13.

6. Jn. 1:17.

7. Gal. 3:19; 1 Tim. 2:5.

8. Deut. 18:15,18; Mk. 1:13; Acts 3:22-23. Author's note: If you want to learn more about these eternal parallels, I refer you to my book, *Principles of Present Truth from Exodus—Deuteronomy* (Richlands, NC: Tabernacle Press, 1983). In it I describe 50 ways in which Moses is a powerful "type" of our Lord.

9. Ex. 4:24-26; compare Gen. 17.

10. Num. 11:24-25.

11. Rom. 8:29; Gal. 4:6; Heb. 2:6-13.

12. Heb. 1:1-3.

13. Ps. 24:1; Rom. 8:17; 1 Pet 3:7.

14. Jer. 51:7-9.

15. Rev. 3:16.

16. Dan. 11:32.

17. Ex. 7:3-4.

18. Ex. 8:19; Lk. 11:20.

19. Ex. 10:16; Num. 33:4.

20. Ex. 18:11; Josh. 2:8-9; 1 Sam. 4:8.

21. Is. 1:6.

22. Rev. 2:11; 20:6,14; 21:8.

23. Ex. 7:12,22; 8:7,18.

24. Is. 26:20-21; 1 Pet 1:5.

25. See Neh. 9:11; Ps. 18:28-29; 66:6,10-12; 84:5-7; 106:7-12; 136:10-18; Is. 48:20-22; 63:13; Jer. 2:6-7; Amos 2:10; Zech. 13:9. Compare the prayer of Jesus in Jn. 17:15.

26. Strong's, #H6395.

27. Strong's, #H6304, H6929, H6923. See Ps. 111:9; 130:7; Is. 50:2.

28. Ruth 3:2; Mt. 13:3-43.

29. Mt. 4:4; 6:11.

30. Jn. 4:14; Col. 1:27.

31. See Jn. 1:29; 1 Cor. 5:7-8; 1 Pet. 1:18-19; Rev. 13:8.

32. Col. 1:9-13; 1 Pet. 2:9-10.

33. See Ex. 14–15.

34. Acts 2:38; Col. 2:11-12.

35. Jn. 12:31; 2 Cor. 4:4.

36. See Acts 1:5; 2:4; 10:46; 19:6.

37. 1 Cor. 12:13.

38. Rom. 8:23; Eph. 1:13-14.

39. Mt. 6:11.

40. Rom. 15:4.

41. Rev. 2:7; 3:22.

42. Strong's, #H4478.

43. See Ex. 16:4; Neh. 9:20; Ps. 78:24-25; 105:40.

44. Ex. 16:16-26.

45. Num. 20:8-12.

46. Col. 1:27; see also Deut. 8:15; Neh. 9:15; Ps. 78:16,20; 105:41; 114:8; Is. 48:21.

47. See Rom. 8:26-27; 1 Cor. 14:2,4,14; Eph. 6:18; Jude 20.

48. Note these chapters: Ex. 18–40; Lev. 1–27; Num. 1–10; and Deut. 4–33.

49. Ps. 103:7.

50. Ex. 19–24.

51. Ex. 25–40.

Chapter Seven

1. Gen. 50:25; Ex. 13:19; Josh. 24:32.

2. Strong's, #G1111. See Mt. 20:11; Lk. 5:30; Jn. 6:41,43,61; 7:32.

3. Strong's, #H596. This word is only used in one other place: Lamentations 3:39.

4. Strong's, #H3885.

5. See Ex. 15:24; 16:2,7-8; 17:3; Num. 14:2,27,29,36; 16:11,41; 17:5; Deut. 1:27.

6. Num. 11:1; Heb. 12:29.

7. Strong's, #H628, H624. Compare Ex. 12:38; Neh. 13:3.

8. Strong's, #H8378, H183.

9. Gal. 5:19-21.

10. 1 Jn. 2:15-17.

11. Strong's #H2600.

12. Gal. 6:7-8.

13. Strong's #H3001.

14. 2 Tim. 4:1-4.

15. Num. 11:34.

16. Ex. 2:15-21; Num. 12:1.

17. This subject and two more "touchy," controversial issues in the Church are covered in depth in my book, *The Three Prejudices* (Shippensburg, PA: Destiny Image, 1997).

18. Mic. 6:4.

19. Num. 12:10.

20. Num. 12:15.

21. Strong's, #G485, G483. See Heb. 6:16; 7:7; 12:3.

22. Compare 1 Chron. 26.

23. Num. 16:3,7,14.

24. Num. 16:20-50.

25. Deut. 1:19-22.

26. Rom. 8:23; Eph. 1:13-14; 4:13.

27. Eph. 1:3; 2:6.

28. Num. 14:1-14,37.

29. Num. 13:33.

30. Num. 14:10.

31. Num. 14:40-45.

32. Acts 7:38.

33. Heb. 2:10.

34. Acts 17:30.

35. Josh. 5:12.

36. Josh. 1:11.

37. Josh. 1:2.

38. See Ex. 32.

39. Strong's, #H3383.

40. 1 Cor. 3:1-15.

41. Josh. 1:12-15.

42. Lk. 18:1.

43. Heb. 10:22,38.

Chapter Eight

1. According to Strong's, the Hebrew word translated as "beautiful" means "to be at home; to be pleasant (or suitable)" (#H4998). It is used twice elsewhere to describe the holiness of His house and the beauty of the Shulamite's cheeks. See Ps. 93:5; Song 1:10.

2. Strong's, #G5611, G5610.

3. Ps. 102:13-16.

4. Strong's, #G2909.

5. "Ointment" in Psalm 133:2 is *shemen*, which is also translated as "anointing" in other places. It means "grease, especially liquid (as from the olive, often perfumed); figuratively, richness" (Strong's, #H8081).

6. Strong's, #H2896.

7. Strong's, #G5048.

8. Strong's, #G5046. See Mt. 5:48; 1 Cor. 13:10; Eph. 4:13; Col. 1:28; 4:12; Heb. 5:14; Jas. 3:2.

9. 1 Jn. 1:1-3.

10. Jn. 1:18.

11. The issues that men raise are covered in my book *The Issues of Life* (Shippensburg, PA: Destiny Image, 1992).

12. See Gen. 27:38-39; Deut. 32:2; Ps. 110:3; Prov. 19:12.

13. Jn. 10:10.

14. Eph. 4:1-3. Unity comes with the *Spirit* of unity.

15. Mk. 3:34-35.

16. Mt. 12:25.

17. 1 Jn. 4:20.

18. Mt. 5:23-24.

19. Eph. 2:14.

20. Gen. 37:1-11; 1 Sam. 17:28.

21. Gen. 13:6-11; Mk. 7:13.

22. 2 Kings 4:40; 2 Cor. 6:7.

23. Jn. 12:32.

24. See Rom. 12:10,16; 1 Jn. 2:8-11; 3:11,23; 4:7-11,19-20.

25. Eph. 4:8-16.

26. Prov. 6:19; Heb. 5:12-14.

27. Mt. 25:40; Acts 9:4; 1 Cor. 11:29; 12:10.

28. Rom. 15:29; Heb. 6:7-8; 1 Pet. 3:8-9.

29. Mt. 5:13-16.

30. Also Rom. 8:34.

31. Col. 1:27.

32. Gen. 3:15; Mt. 1:1.

33. Ps. 72:8,17,19.

34. Compare Is. 60; Rev. 21–22.

35. The word used here is *tephillah*, and it means "intercession, supplication, a hymn." Its root word means "to judge (officially or mentally); by extension, to intercede, pray" (Strong's, #H8605, H6419).

36. Strong's, #H3615.

37. Mt. 16:18.

38. Amos 3:3; Jas. 1:8.

39. Num. 14:21; Ps. 72:19; Hab. 2:14.

Chapter Nine

1. We are told by the apostle Paul that "...in Him [Jesus Christ] dwelleth *all the fulness* of the Godhead bodily" (Col. 2:9; see also 1:19). To properly communicate the absolute unity and intimacy of the relationship between God the Father, God the Son, and God the Holy Spirit, I must walk right up to the edge of "Oneness" or the "Jesus only" doctrine. This may alarm some readers and please those of my brethren who are indeed of the "Oneness" persuasion, but Jesus has prayed that you and I will share the unity He shares with His Father. At times they are so close as to be virtually indistinguishable and indivisible. Would to God that we would quickly become the same! It is my conviction that our Creator is well aware of our mental and spiritual limitations, including our inability to fully grasp His triune nature and absolute unity as "the one God." As long as we seek Him in sincerity and truth, He will answer in mercy and grace and "explain" the details later face to face.

2. Eph. 4:3,13.

3. Song 1:1.

4. Strong's, #H7381.

5. Strong's, #H7306.

6. Lk. 4:18; Acts 10:38.

7. Col. 1:19; 2:9.

8. Col. 2:11-12.

9. Gal. 3:27.

10. Ex. 20:7; Prov. 30:9.

11. Strong's, #H410.

12. Ps. 18:1-2; Lk. 1:51; Rev. 5:12.

13. Phil. 1:19.

14. Strong's, #H430.

15. Strong's, #H433.

16. Compare Eph. 3:9; Col. 1:16-17; Heb. 1:2-3; Rev. 4:11.

17. 1 Cor. 1:24.

18. Strong's, #H7706.

19. Strong's, #H7703.

20. Strong's, #H7699.

21. Compare Tit. 3:5; Heb. 2:17; 5:2.

22. Jn. 14:6; 1 Cor. 13:13.

23. 1 Jn. 3–4.

24. Jn. 13:34-35.

25. Strong's, #H5945.

26. Strong's, #H5927.

27. Strong's, #H5930.

28. Ps. 110:4; Heb. 5–7.

29. Mt. 28:18.

30. Dan. 7:18-27; Rev. 3:21.

Chapter Ten

1. Strong's, #H3068. According to the same source, *Yehovah* (translated as "Lord") appears 7125 times in 6011 verses of the Old Testament.

2. Strong's, #H1961.

3. Jn. 1:1-18; 8:58.

4. Compare the "I AM's" of Jesus found in the Gospel of John (see Jn. 6:35; 8:12,58; 10:9; 11:25; 14:6; 15:1).

5. Ps. 89.

6. Rev. 17:14.

7. Rev. 2:10.

8. Strong's, #H3070.

9. Phil. 4:19. See also Ruth 2:1; Ps. 23:1; Lk. 12:30-33; Eph. 1:18; 2:7; 3:8.

10. Gen. 22:13.

11. See Rom. 12:4-5; 1 Cor. 12:12-27; Eph. 4:25; 5:30; and Heb. 4:16; 1 Jn. 3:17.

12. Strong's, #H7495.

13. Jn. 10:10.

14. 1 Thess. 5:23.

15. See Mt. 10:8; Mk. 16:15-20; Lk. 9:2; 10:9.

16. Strong's, #H3071, H5251.

17. Jn. 3:14; 12:32-33.

18. Col. 2:15; 1 Jn. 3:8; compare Mt. 12:20; 1 Cor. 15:54-57.

19. Ex. 17:12-13.

20. 1 Jn. 5:4; Rev. 15:2.

21. Strong's, #H6942.

22. Jn. 19:34.

23. Jn. 18:38; 19:4-6; Heb. 7:26; compare Rom. 1:4; Heb. 12:10,14.

24. Eph. 5:25-27; Heb. 13:12.

25. Is. 56:4.

26. Strong's, #H3073, H7965.

27. Is. 9:6; Heb. 7:2.

28. Col. 1:20.

29. Rom. 14:17.

30. Rom. 8:6.

31. Rom. 16:20; Eph. 4:3.

32. Strong's, #H8199.

33. Jn. 5:22; Rom. 2:16; 2 Tim. 4:1,8.

34. Jn. 16:8-11.

35. Mt. 2:6; Rev. 1:5; 19:16.

36. 1 Cor. 6:1-3.

37. Mt. 7:1-5; Jn. 7:24.

38. 1 Cor. 11:26-31; 2 Cor. 13:5; Gal. 6:4.

39. 1 Cor. 12:10.

40. Is. 61:6; Rev. 1:6; 5:10.

41. Strong's, #H6664.

42. Heb. 1:8.

43. 2 Cor. 5:21.

44. Compare 2 Tim. 2:22; 3:16; Heb. 11:33; 12:11; Jas. 3:18; 2 Pet. 1:1; Rev. 19:8.

45. Strong's, #H7462.

46. Jn. 10:11-14; Heb. 13:20; 1 Pet. 5:4; compare Ps. 80:1; Ezek. 34:23; 37:24; 1 Pet. 2:25.

47. Is. 40:11; 1 Pet. 5:7.

48. Ezek. 36:38; Jn. 10:16.

49. Ps. 79:13; also Ps. 95:7; 100:3.

50. 1 Cor. 12:25; compare 2 Cor. 8:16; Phil. 4:10.

51. Eph. 4:11.

52. Strong's, #H6213.

53. Strong's, #H3766 and H1288, respectively.

54. Jn. 8:29.

55. Phil. 2:5-11.

56. Rev. 5:12-13.

57. Jn. 4:23-24.

58. Phil. 2:5.

59. Compare Prov. 15:33; 22:4; Jas. 4:6,10—and the ministries of Eph. 4:11.

60. Phil. 2:10.

61. Strong's, #H8033.

62. 1 Cor. 2:8; Col. 1:19; 2:9.

63. See Jn. 1:14-18; 14:1-2; Heb. 1:1-3; 2:9.

64. Jn. 17:20-24; Rom. 8:18; 11:36.

65. Hag. 2:9.

66. 2 Cor. 3:18; compare Eph. 1:18; 3:16,21; Phil. 3:21.

67. Col. 1:27; compare Col. 3:4; 1 Thess. 2:12; Heb. 2:10-11; 1 Pet. 5:4; 2 Pet. 1:3; Rev. 21:23-26.

68. Gen. 37:3.

69. Strong's, #G4182.

70. Strong's, #G4164.

71. Strong's, #G2819, G3551.

72. Rev. 3:12.

73. 2 Pet. 1:4.

Chapter Eleven

1. Is. 66:8.

2. Heb. 11:4.

3. Eph. 1:9-11.

4. Heb. 12:25-29.

5. Strong's, #G2347. See Acts 14:22; Rom. 8:29.

6. 1 Cor. 10:1-4.

7. Joseph the patriarch's life ended as it began, within the predetermined confines of sovereign grace, a "coffin" as it were that represents a total death to self (Gen. 50:26).

8. Deut. 28:13.

9. Strong's, #G2307, G2309.

10. Jesus is the "Pattern Son" because He is the firstborn of many brethren, and the Author and Finisher of our faith (Rom. 8:29; Heb. 12:2).

11. Strong's, #G4243, G4245.

12. Mt. 5:9.

13. Mt. 12:30.

14. For a full historical and biblical treatment of these deadly principalities, see my book, *The Three Prejudices* (Shippensburg, PA: Destiny Image, 1997).

15. Strong's, #G4798, G4862, G5530.

16. Lk. 10:33; 17:16; Jn. 8:48.

17. 1 Kings 11–12.

18. Strong's, #G2873. See 1 Cor. 15:58; 2 Cor. 11:23,27; 1 Thess. 1:3; 2:9.

19. Heb. 6:10.

20. Jn. 2:10.

21. Gen. 50:25; Ex. 13:19; Josh. 24:32.

22. Mt. 27:51-52.

23. 2 Kings 13:21.

24. Song 6:13.

25. 1 Thess. 4:13-18.

26. Mt. 24:31.

27. Is. 40:3; Mt. 3:3.

28. I would also admonish the saints to stop casually coming into the house of the Lord without ever "paying" for their spiritual meal. Many of our folks are what we in the South would describe as being "as full as a tick" (they're so full they've puffed up to twice their size). Without a thought, they get up and walk out the door without paying the servant of God his due, let alone leaving a tip! God's Word admonishes us that "the labourer is worthy of his hire," and that we should never "muzzle the mouth of the ox" who grinds the corn. An elder who labors in the Word to feed God's flock is worthy of a "double honour" or stipend (Lk. 10:7; 1 Cor. 9:7-9; 1 Tim. 5:17).

29. Jn. 3:6.

30. 1 Cor. 6:17; Heb. 12:9.

31. 2 Cor. 5:16.

32. Song 5:10-16.

33. Strong's, #G4029.

34. That is the Hebrew word *massa'*, which means "a burden; figuratively, an utterance" (Strong's, #4853). It is also translated in the King James Version as "song" (1 Chron. 15:22,27) and "prophecy" (Prov. 30:1; 31:1).

35. See also Lk. 10:2.

Chapter Twelve

1. Strong's, #G2212.

2. Eph. 4:16.

3. Mt. 18:20.

4. Eph. 5:21.

5. Eph. 4:26.

6. Rom. 4; Gal. 3:14,29.

7. Strong's, #H1419.

8. 1 Cor. 12:18 says, "But now hath *God set the members every one of them in the body*, as it hath pleased Him."

9. 1 Cor. 1:10.

10. 1 Cor. 12:6.

11. 1 Cor. 12:18,28.

12. Job 22:28.

13. Ps. 75:6-7.

14. 1 Sam. 15:22-23.

15. The "horns" or corners of the mercy seat were sprinkled with the blood of sacrificed "sin offerings" by the high priest under the Old Covenant, signifying the blood of the sacrificed Lamb of God, Jesus Christ, who would take away the sins of the world (Ex. 30:6-10; Jn. 1:29).

16. Ex. 33:23.

17. 2 Cor. 4:6.

18. Song 4:12-16.

19. Strong's, #G1997. See Mt. 23:37; 24:31; Mk. 1:33; 13:27; Lk. 12:1; 13:34; 17:37; 2 Thess. 2:1.

20. Ps. 122:3; Eph. 4:16.

21. Strong's, #G1922.

22. Ps. 139:14.

23. Joel 1:10,17.

24. Job 14:14.

25. Strong's, #G3868. See Heb. 12:25.

26. 2 Cor. 2:17.

27. This is the only true fulfillment of His call of the apostle, prophet, evangelist, pastor, and teacher according to Ephesians 4:12. We are given to the Church by Jesus to perfect (or "thoroughly furnish and equip") the saints *for the work of the ministry....*

28. Is. 52:14.

29. Ps. 110:1; also Heb. 10:12-13.

30. Acts 3:19-21.

31. Joel 2:25.

32. Eph. 4:13.

33. Joel 2:28-32; Jas. 5:7.

34. Rev. 14:1-5.

35. Strong's, #H6891, especially #H6868.

Books and Tapes By Kelley Varner

Tape Catalog

To receive a full listing of Pastor Varner's books and tapes, or information about our Tape of the Month and Seminars or Conventions, write or call for our current catalog:

Praise Tabernacle
P.O. Box 785
Richlands, NC 28574-0785
Phone: (910) 324-5026 or 324-5027
FAX: (910) 324-1048
E-mail: kvarner@nternet.net
Internet: www.kelleyvarner.com

Other exciting titles
by Kelley Varner

━━━ PREVAIL—A HANDBOOK FOR THE OVERCOMER
ISBN 0-938612-06-9

━━━ THE MORE EXCELLENT MINISTRY
ISBN 0-914903-60-8

━━━ THE PRIESTHOOD IS CHANGING
ISBN 1-56043-033-8

━━━ UNDERSTANDING TYPES, SHADOWS & NAMES, VOLS. 1 & 2
The first two volumes in a series, they examine the main definition of a biblical term, its themes, how Christ fulfilled it, and how it applies to Christianity.
Vol. 1 ISBN 1-56043-165-2   Vol. 2 ISBN 1-56043-197-0

━━━ MOSES, THE MASTER, AND THE MANCHILD
Discover how Moses, our Lord Jesus, and the mighty victorious Church of the last days paint a picture of hope, power, and glory for God's people. You will be left breathless as Kelley Varner cuts through the confusion and fear surrounding the times in which we live.
ISBN 0-7684-2121-7

━━━ WHOSE RIGHT IT IS
Here Pastor Varner carefully examines the Scriptures for a proper perspective on Christ's Lordship and dispensationalism.
ISBN 1-56043-151-2

━━━ REST IN THE DAY OF TROUBLE
This book studies in detail the prophecy of Habakkuk. We too are in a day of trouble and, like Habakkuk, can we find rest in ours?
ISBN 1-56043-119-9

━━━ THE THREE PREJUDICES
Three walls of prejudice are still blocking God's power from flowing as freely and as strongly as He desires. Learn the truth from the Bible about gender, race, and nations!
ISBN 1-56043-187-3

━━━ UNSHAKEABLE PEACE
In a detailed study of the Book of Haggai, Pastor Varner presents the *unshakeable peace* that characterizes the Church that Jesus is building!
ISBN 1-56043-137-7

━━━ THE TIME OF THE MESSIAH
There are four characteristics of the Messiah's first coming. Can you recognize these same signs in our present season—the season of the Holy Spirit upon the Church?
ISBN 1-56043-177-6

Available at your local Christian bookstore.

For more information and sample chapters, visit www.destinyimage.com

5B-3:141